HIDDEN HISTORY

of

CAMBRIDGE & HARVARD

HIDDEN HISTORY
of
CAMBRIDGE & HARVARD

JANE MERRILL

THE
History
PRESS

Published by The History Press
Charleston, SC
www.historypress.com

First published 2023

Manufactured in the United States

ISBN 9781467152679

Library of Congress Control Number: 2023934796

CONTENTS

PREFACE

There are always things hidden before our very eyes that reveal the past. Elizabeth Peabody, an early Transcendentalist and sister-in-law of Nathaniel Hawthorne, explained accidentally walking into a tree: "I saw it, but I did not realize it." Strolling around Cambridge and Harvard for this book, I had no test to take or jobs to show up for. Rather, in a sense, I walked into trees on purpose, my principal aims being to satisfy my curiosity and the reader's, in a town and university saturated with history. Of these experiences of seeing, hearing and imagining what was hidden in full view, a sample point of interest is a length of seawall between Winthrop and Eliot Streets and the Town Creek.

Only six months after the settlement of the town, in 1631, all the towns in Massachusetts Colony were assessed for dredging and widening the Town Creek, so promising a commercial route as it appeared to connect with the Charles River. This drained the pens of village cattle, bordered the town cemetery and ran through Harvard Square. By 1636, it had a landing stage and a ferry, but Cambridge was not destined to be a river port. Ships grounded in it at low tide, and both Boston and Charleston had better ports, thus the Town Creek canal was eventually filled in with ash.

However, between 1793 and 1811, a ten-foot-high dry-laid retaining wall was constructed here of granite and Roxbury puddingstone. One person in a million who passed by in our era had any awareness of it until Charles Sullivan, director of the Cambridge Historical Commission, applied to the city for an application to restore the wall. In Sullivan's view,

Historic stone retaining wall (Winthrop Wall), visible behind a fire hydrant, from Eliot Street, photo 1909. *Cambridge Historical Commission, Boston Elevated Railway Collection.*

it dates from around 1800 and reflects a plan not realized to create a wall, and perhaps a wharf, on the Town Creek to take advantage of the newly opened Middlesex Canal. This would have brought waterborne commerce to the area around Harvard. Part of the wall is currently in disrepair, but there are plans for its restoration. The commission considers it a permanent part of the landscape.

The Middlesex Canal was a wonder of its time—a twenty-seven-mile waterway with a Revolutionary War veteran as chief engineer, as well as his five sons working under him. Loammi Baldwin, born in Woburn, Massachusetts, where a fine statue of him stands today, is considered the father of American civil engineering. As a young man, Baldwin, with his best friend Benjamin Thompson, inspired by the experiments of Benjamin Franklin, had walked from Woburn to the classes of Professor Winthrop at Harvard. Working with his sons to complete the job of the canal, Baldwin invented ingenious apparatuses, such as the first dump truck. Thompson, a Loyalist, was likewise an engineer and, after fleeing the Massachusetts Colony for Europe, invented processes and things from the crouton to the smoke-free fireplace. The two young men were not of a status to afford Harvard College and beside which had no wish to be ministers, but the atmosphere of learning lit ambition in them. Like many students in this college town over four centuries, they must have thought what the seventeenth-century English thought: "What shall I do to be forever known, and make the coming age my own."

ACKNOWLEDGMENTS

For the knowledge and enthusiasm of the following persons, the author expresses lasting gratitude.

Louise Ambler, Archivist, Christ Church, Cambridge.

Tim Driscoll, Archivist, Harvard University.

Chris Filstrup, Director of the Stony Brook University Libraries.

Meta Partenheimer, Archivist, Cambridge Historical Commission.

Kit Rawlins, Assistant Director, Cambridge Historical Commission.

Marieke Van Damme, Executive Director, History Cambridge.

Part I

EARLY YEARS

THE FOUNDING

Unquestionably, the ministers of the Massachusetts Bay Colony were driven to keep the flocks in line, to curb tendencies to splintering. The Puritans purified the Church of England of papism and resisted interference in the New World. The synods that met in early Cambridge were so repressive that a body might have wanted to run—not walk—to more tolerant Providence, Rhode Island.

The founding of Harvard had a link to purging the Massachusetts Colony of disseminating elements. The Great and General Courts rotated in session between Boston and Cambridge. John Winthrop led the settlement of 1630, and Anne Hutchinson arrived in 1636, the year after Harvard was founded. Winthrop, the first governor, was a religious idealist, while Hutchinson continued the mission of radical lay preacher that she had set herself in England. She questioned the sermons of the colonial ministers, conducted meetings in her home and preached grace as opposed to strict governance by the clergy and law. Additionally, she practiced midwifery, something of which she had intimate knowledge from having given birth to eleven children. Winthrop called Hutchinson a "woman of ready wit and a bold spirit"[1] who brought over dangerous ideas.

Were it not for outbreaks of disease, two-hour sermons and witch hunting, early Cambridge would have been a paradise. William Wood, an ironmaster who immigrated from overseas during the Great Migration, described

Embroidered view of Harvard Hall. Silk, wool and gilt-silver yarns on open plain-weave linen attributed to Mary Leverett Denison Rogers, circa early eighteenth century. *Massachusetts Historical Society.*

Newtowne (the original name for Cambridge) as one of the neatest and best compacted towns in New England, "having many fair structures with many handsome contrived streets. The inhabitants most of them are very rich and well-stored with cattell of all sorts. On the other side of the river lieth all their medow and march-ground for hay." What the inhabitants thought lacking was an institution of learning, which they rapidly went about establishing.[2]

SYNODS

A synod of ministers in November 1737 identified eighty-three erroneous opinions held by Anne Hutchinson. Her trial, about fourteen months after the founding of Harvard, was held in Cambridge and attended by the clerics of the colony. Governor Henry Vane, then age twenty-four, an advocate of religious freedom and tolerance, declared Hutchinson innocent, but Winthrop's side prevailed and she was banished. Five of her older children remained in New England, while she settled with the young ones near Split Rock, now the Bronx, New York. She and five younger children were killed during the conflict called Kief's War (1642–45), when a New Amsterdam military officer began a war with native tribes in New York and New Jersey. Of Hutchinson's children, only nine-year-old Susanna survived and was taken captive.

Right: Turned great chair, three-legged European ash with American oak pommels, circa 1550–1600. First used by Reverend Edward Holyoke, president, 1737–69. *Harvard Art Museums.*

Below: Harvard Square with fence. *Harvard University Archives.*

That Henry Vane held to his belief that Anne Hutchinson was a good and innocent woman indicates that although the ministers at the Puritan synods stood together in condemning her, the populace had divergent and more liberal views. A university was just the ticket to gather up boys from good families and commit them to the ruling Puritan code. The reason why Winthrop decided to have the trial in Cambridge was that Boston was more a merchants' town, whereas Cambridge was already a smart address with more reactionary property holders.

The Massachusetts Colony had established Harvard College with a timely burst of money from the British missionary society. Without adequate funds, a university could come to naught, which is what happened to the Loyalists' dream of a great university to rival Harvard in New Brunswick after they fled the lower colonies during the War for Independence.

GOVERNOR WINTHROP

The namesakes of Harvard's Winthrop House are effectively two. John Winthrop led the first settlement to Massachusetts—one hundred people in the *Arabella*, of the thirteen-ship convoy called the Winthrop Fleet, in 1630. He and Thomas Dudley rowed up the river and climbed a hill on the north shore. This is where Dudley declared that this was the spot for the capital of the Massachusetts Colony. It is at the corner of JFK and Mount Auburn Streets.

Winthrop became the colony's first governor. The *Arabella* carried ten thousand gallons of wine and a stock of three time as much beer as water. While strict in their behavior, the Puritans condoned alcohol.

It is well known that fame leads to becoming the namesake of places and products the namesakes would never imagine. Winthrop, Massachusetts, a peninsula, belonged to Pawtucket Indians until the Puritans chose to settle there. They called the place Pulling Point because of the brisk tides that made for hard rowing, and it became the most densely populated town in the Boston area around whose docks are stinging jelly fish for those who try to swim there.

There was a lot of jockeying for lands and jurisdictions by the colonists. The settlers led by John Winthrop built a palisade one and a half miles north of what is today's Cambridge Common. There were seventy or so houses close together, and Newtowne was wealthy, as proved by the fact that it paid the highest taxes in the colonies. Before it grew, the settlement fragmented. First the leader, Winthrop, decided that he preferred Boston. He and Deputy Governor Dudley quarreled over the expensive wainscotting that Dudley used on his house. According to Winthrop, the panels were too expensive, but Dudley thought this décor in good taste, and probably, appropriate as an insulation.

Reverend Thomas Hooker was Cambridge's first minister. He arrived in Boston in 1633. His sermons lasted more than two hours. Cotton Mather called him the "Light of the Western Churches." Hooker also stirred unrest. Some of his parishioners were impressed by the lands around the Connecticut River. They felt that they had too little meadow land for their cows in Newtowne and wanted to depart. The handy official reason they gave was that territories south (Connecticut) would otherwise fall into the hands of the Dutch or another group of English colonists. At the General Court, Hooker's congregation pleaded the strong bent of their spirits to remove thither. In 1635, Hooker and his fifty families set out on an exodus on foot, following an old Native American trail from Charleston one hundred miles through the wilderness of Connecticut to found Hartford.

Newtowne had eighty-five houses basically laid out on a grid. Thomas Dudley advanced from lieutenant governor to governor while the General Courts of the colony were held in Newtowne; for many years in the mid-1600s, he was the British colonial governor. The town was already receiving compliments for being pleasant and neat, thought to outdo Boston itself. Between 1629 and 1650, Dudley was elected deputy governor of the colony thirteen times and served as governor four times. He would have been a gentleman in favor of beautifying Newtowne.

DISCORD

The Massachusetts Bay Colony was built on a base of one thousand Puritans. Thomas Dudley aimed to make Newtowne/Cambridge its noble capital, hence early settlers had a church with a bell. New Englanders may have looked at Cambridge as a backwater in a positive sense, safe from Native American opposition and from pirates. The fifty families of Reverend Hooker drove their cattle before them as they traveled and founded Hartford.

The Common was established in 1631. Stray livestock would be housed in a sort of stone pen until the owner claimed them. Fine houses had been built west of present-day Harvard Square by 1700, of which some survive, the oldest being the Cooper-Frost-Austin House, built by church deacon and town selectman Samuel Cooper in 1681 in the English Medieval lean-to style. It has a two-story façade with a one-story real elevation connected by a long sloping room, or catside. It is reasonable to picture other houses of this form in the town, as well as squirrels and cats scampering up and down them.

A General Court was called together from the colonies to establish a church government and discipline. One rousing feature was John Eliot's sermon, preached to members of the Massachusett tribe before the whole assembly and legislature on June 9, 1647, shortly after his first sermon to them. Eliot was understood to be a holy person. He had a degree from Jesus College of Cambridge, England, and then tutored in a school kept by Thomas Hooker. (Of Hooker's family, Eliot said while they were in England, "When I came to this blessed family I then saw as never before a power of godliness in its lovely vigour and efficacy.[3]) His meeting house in Roxbury, southwest of Boston for nearly sixty years, was a rude log cabin with a thatched roof. To the Puritans, the congregation were the visible saints, so there was no justification to reserve a house for public assembly for divine service. Cotton Mather said that he once heard Eliot say these remarkable words in response to a statement that the conversation of the faithful is in heaven:

In the evening if we ask, "where have I been today?", our souls must answer, "in heaven." If thou art a believer, thou art no stranger to heaven while thou livest, and when thou diest, heaven will be no stranger to thee; no, thou hast been there a thousand times before.[4]

Eliot often walked to his "Praying Indians" on the south side of the river, in Nonantum, now part of Newton, to preach. One year before he preached to the Cambridge assembly, he had begun to preach to the Indian settlement. He made converts, and a few of the youth were educated, which sparked the building of an Indian college at Cambridge. Regarding the lives of his flock, Eliot was as severe as the hardcore Puritans in Cambridge when it came to heresy. As there were quite a few—Quakers, Anabaptists, the followers of Anne Hutchinson and the Familists, the Dutch sect known as "The Family of Love"—clearly the Puritans guarded their dominance tightly, and Eliot thought that unorthodox views were creeping into the community.

He recorded his judgments in his parish book: for example, about a sneaky baker's wife who nipped off bits from each loaf and two servants who went to the oyster bank against the counsel of their "governor," left their boat afloat and drowned when the tide carried it away—an example of God's displeasure against obstinate servants. Eliot also preached against the fashion of long hair and wigs. Harvard college laws of 1655 declared that students must wear no ruffles or gold or silver ornaments unless the president personally approved them and that it was unlawful to wear locks or foretops, as well as to use curling, cropping, parting or powdering.

In the era of the Salem witches, it is not so astounding that a woman was said to have been put to death in Cambridge for the crime of witchcraft in 1650, nor that an enslaved woman was burned at the stake in Cambridge in 1740 for allegedly poisoning her master.

Harvard's First President

Religion was at the fore of the education at the college. One can't help wondering if there really were Hebrew scholars of the Bible as claimed. The first president, Henry Dunster, was supposed to be one such linguist. In office as president from 1640 to 1655, he was a minister, and so were the next six presidents. Dunster was educated at Cambridge University in England. He immigrated to America to escape persecution for nonconformity. The Puritans, now calling themselves Congregationalists, welcomed him to take over from Master Nathaniel Eaton, judged to be overly severe. But Dunster, though universally liked, was induced to resign after fourteen years on a theological point. Not only did Dunster question the validity of infant baptism, but he also neglected the baptism of his own children due to his "believer baptism."[5]

Like Henry Dunster, Benanuel Bower (1627–1798) did not expect persecution when he left Lincolnshire, England, for the colonies. He and his wife, Elizabeth Dunster, were from Lancashire. They both had immigrated to Massachusetts by about 1653. There they raised a family of four sons and seven daughters. Benanuel belonged to the Society of Friends when he departed England. It may be that Elizabeth came as an orphan and converted, or she might have dwelt with her uncle Henry Dunster for a while in Scituate or Cambridge.

In 1655, the ruling body of the colony banned Quakers under penalty of death. The Puritans/Congregationalists were deadly serious. In 1656, two Quakers were hanged in Boston, and Elizabeth and Benanuel, whose house

Above: *View in Cambridge*, 1830, by James Kidder, *Appleton's Journal*, March 5, 1870. Cattle continued to be driven through Harvard Square to the Brighton slaughterhouse into the 1920s. *University of Michigan.*

Right: J.S. Copley, Colonel Brattle, Harvard Art Museums/Fogg Museum. Partial gift of Mrs. Thomas Brattle Gannett and partial purchase through the generosity of Robert T. Gannett, an anonymous donor and the Alpheus Hyatt Purchasing Fund. *President and Fellows of Harvard College, 1978.*

served for meetings, were apparently attacked there around this time and were admonished by the county court in the fall of 1663. Ursula Cole, one of the women identified as attending a Quaker meeting at the Bowers', had boldly reviled two ministers at Charlestown. The court inadvertently gave the Quakers a platform for their beliefs and opinions, such as comparing caterwauling to a Puritan sermon.

A Quaker went four times to the Boston court for permission to buy a house. The Quaker position was that the king had promised that the Quakers could enjoy liberty in his overseas plantations. The Quaker was denied and thrown into a dark prison without bread or water for two days and nights. Benanuel Bower brought the jailed Quaker a jug of milk and was cast into prison too for entertaining a stranger. Meanwhile, the Quaker's defense was clear as a bell: that he was weary and depleted, and if he had come to the prosecutor's house, he ought to have been given hospitality instead of being whipped. Likewise, Elizabeth Bower and one of her daughters, also named Elizabeth, were arrested for attending a Friends meeting and whipped; another daughter, Barbara, was driven to Boston tied to the tail of a cart.

Benanuel Bower was fined year after year and seems to have been indomitable. He wrote a poem against Thomas Danforth as his principal tormentor and accused him publicly at the close of a church service. This was incredibly brave considering that Danforth, who lived on Kirkland Street, was the largest landholder in the colony, having over fifteen thousand acres of farmland to the west of Cambridge, and held many offices of the town, from college treasurer to judge of the Supreme Court from 1692 to his death in 1699. Danforth oversaw the Salem witch trials of 1692 to 1693.

Identifying himself as a man of sixty who lived one mile from the center of Cambridge, Benanuel wrote from Cambridge Prison on March 24, 1677, that he had been assaulted during a Friends meeting, hauled out of the room by his heels, down some stairs and carried on a wheelbarrow to prison.

Several of the Bowers' daughters were prompted by the anti-Quaker persecution to move to Philadelphia, where Quakers had more acceptance. Meanwhile, the first president of Harvard College navigated for some years a safe course, and fortunately for Harvard, he had this august place in its governance. When the college was founded by a vote of the court in 1636 (and opened in 1638) as the earliest college in the colonies, Nathaniel Eaton, a slaveholder, became the schoolmaster in charge when the college opened in 1638. Eaton was dismissed for misuse of funds and harsh discipline, and Henry Dunster was appointed president, holding that office until 1655. The Bowers already had five children in 1658 when her uncle

Henry Dunster left a bequest of five shillings apiece to his cousin and her children. It is fascinating that Henry Dunster had high status as president of the only college in the colonies yet critiqued the dominant faith and did not break with his cousin despite her open adherence to the Society of Friends. Downplaying his unorthodox views would have been safer. An earnest classicist and admired Hebrew scholar, Dunster was asked to assist the translator of the Psalms to revise a translation from Hebrew that became the *New England Psalm Book* of 1740. He was not removed from issues of his day. He rubbed shoulders with dangerous heresy, the libertarian views of both Baptists and Quakers. There were different sects in a theological setting of entrenched positions, as well as sympathizers of more liberal views, factors multiplying the diversity of faiths.

When ousted, Dunster self-exiled to the church in Scituate, where he had preached years before. Despite modest means, he gave one hundred acres to the needy college in his will and asked to be buried close to the college he loved. Dunster's grave site is at the old Burying Yard, a stone's throw from Harvard Yard, which inspired Longfellow to write the poem "God's Acre":

> *I like that ancient Saxon phrase, which calls*
> *The burial-ground God's-Acre! It is just;*
> *It consecrates each grave within its walls,*
> *And breathes a benison o'er the sleeping dust.*

The Anglicans had probably elected Dunster the president of the college knowing that he had divergent views, but who didn't like to debate religion in Cambridge? It was worth it to him to keep his doubts about the Puritans in his vest pocket to fulfill his ambition for a liberal university in the European tradition.

Reverend Dunster outlined Harvard's educational scope in the charter. As the missionaries had to be pleased in the opening of colonial colleges, to make them tax exempt and bring in students preparing for the ministry, the charter expressly states that the college "may conduce to the education of the English and Indian youth of the country." Also, the liberal arts, as in British universities, rather than just religion, was endorsed in the charter. And "any well devoted persons" were moved to "bestow sundry gifts, legacies, lands, and revenues for the advancement of all good literature, arts, and sciences in Harvard College."[6] After six presidents had come and gone, Increase Mather, the seventh, tried to bring the purpose of the college from opening minds to pure religion. He met with little success.

Mather was in London soliciting funds for the college when the witch trials began. Even a minister, Reverend George Burroughs (class of 1670), was seized. From June, more than two hundred persons were accused, and twenty men and women were hanged or stoned to death. As the executions began, Increase effectively became a voice of reason. He read a paper to the Cambridge ministers (later published as "Cases of Conscience Concerning Evil Spirits"). It denounced spectral evidence and asserted that it was better to let Satan have his way with a dozen people than have one innocent die. Mather's paper broke the back of the persecution and brought the authorities to the side of reason and clemency. However, Cotton Mather, Increase Mather's son, had participated in the mania and was exposed and denounced a few years after the trials. Legend has it that Increase collected the copies of the book that cast his son in a poor light as a hardline witch hunter and burned them in a bonfire in the yard. This would prove the only book burning incident in Harvard history.

Printing in Old Cambridge

Printing and bookshops are enduring features of Cambridge. Harvard University Press remains, and the goddess Athena, an eighteen-foot gilded sculpture executed by Adio diBiccari, still sits on top of the old Athenaeum Press plant at 215 First Street, East Cambridge, and can be seen from the Charles River and the Longfellow Bridge.

The arrival of the first printing press in the American colonies in 1638 marked the start of an indelible connection between Harvard College (founded two years before) and Cambridge. The press was brought by Reverend Joseph Glover, a Puritan who quit his rectorship in Sutton, Surrey, England, along with his wife, Elizabeth, and their children, as well as a Mr. Stephen Dayes, to join the 1630 colony led by John Winthrop. Stephen Dayes was a locksmith, which then meant all-round mechanic, hired to operate the press. He was supposed to repay Glover the cost of passage, but when Glover died during the voyage, Dayes's debt was transferred to the minister's widow. Now owner of the printing press, she launched a print shop with Dayes. The press when constructed was six feet high with a base a yard long, so presumably it had its own room in the president's frame house in Harvard Yard. The press was the same form of wooden hand press as adapted from the wine press in the 1400s, used until the invention of the all-iron presses.

Their first years in Cambridge, Stephen Dayes and his son, Matthew, were very busy. They issued a broadside and an almanac and eventually a bound book. Elizabeth was an eligible woman of property and soon (1641) was wed to Henry Dunster, a person of considerable prestige as president of Harvard College. Soon the press, as well as eleven featherbeds formerly the property of Reverend Glover, resided in the Dunster House and was under Harvard's control; it became officially college property by 1658.

Matthew Dayes, who had superior workmanship, died at twenty-nine. A third printer, his successor, was Samuel Green, who had come in 1630 with John Winthrop and Thomas Dudley. Green had nineteen children by two wives and was the commander of the Cambridge militia, while managing the press, for fifty years. Green seeded printers all over New England, accounting for the beautiful printing of early New England. One of his sons, Bartholomew, founded the first newspaper, the *News Letter*, in 1704, and another, Timothy, became the second printer of Connecticut. Early publications were somewhat crude and of local use, like the *Bay Psalms*, 1640 (a metrical translation); *Theses at the Commencement of Harvard College*, 1648; *The Book of General Lawes and Libertyes*, 1648; and *Spiritual Milk for Boston Babes*, 1656. All are very rare today. John Eliot coauthored the *Bay Psalms* with other Puritans; he wished that the psalms be sung, not recited in church. Ten complete copies of it are extant, with one each held at the Bodleian Library and the New York Public Library. During the fall of 1650, Green issued for Eliot an Indian translation of a portion of the Psalms in the Algonquian language of the Massachusett tribe. Two last items printed by Green alone were broadsides: "An Humble Proposal for the Inlargement of University of Learning in New England" and "A Declaration of the General Court... Concerning the Execution of two Quakers," both printed in 1659.

Much religious zeal of Protestants in England went to converting indigenous American people. This coincided with the innovation of the Bible translated from Latin to English. Martin Luther receives credit for this enterprise; he believed that whatever language was spoken, the Bible should be in that language. But the brilliant scholar William Tyndale was burned alive when he refused to recant his English-language Bible in the mid-1500s. In the 1600s, Bibles in the vernacular had the imprimatur of royalty, resulting in the scholarly group effort of the King James Bible.

As for John Eliot, the pastor arrived in the Commonwealth of Massachusetts in 1631 during the Great Migration; he had begun the study of the language of the Massachusett tribe a decade later when he settled in the woods of Natick, west of Cambridge, as a missionary. The Society

1833 lithograph: "View of the ancient buildings belonging to Harvard College."
Bridgeman Images.

for the Propagation of the Gospel was a powerful missionary force and supported the edition of Eliot's translation of the Geneva Bible. Printed in Cambridge, first the New Testament in 1661 and both Old and New in 1663, it was a mammoth enterprise for Harvard's press and a dazzling feat to have accomplished in fourteen years. Eliot had the help of the Natick tribe, and not unexpectedly, he devised an Algonquian dictionary and grammar along the way.

While conversion was Eliot's goal, he recognized the native population as intelligent. He was not aiming to take their land and did not consider them primitive. They were God's people and deserved the gospel like anyone else. He was admired by some of the leaders of Cambridge, and Harvard's president came out to hear his sermons. Soon, a faster press was needed. Harvard got a new assistant for Green, and the Gospel Society in London sent a new printing press in the fall of 1650, as well as a Mr. Marmaduke Johnson, who worked with Eliot and on other projects. Johnson printed fifty nine books, pamphlets and broadsides in Cambridge, twenty in cooperation with Samuel Green and in the Indian College with Johnson. He was the first skilled typesetter in English America. His name is associated with some of the best early printing of the colonies but also with scandal, as Johnson got into debt, overly imbibed and, it was said, frolicked with Green's daughter even though he had left a wife in London. Eliot by contrast was unblemished.

His ardent sermons engaged Native Americans and brought Puritans in Cambridge out to listen.

As for bookshops, combining them with cafés has been an innovation of the late twentieth century. Cambridge once had well over a dozen bookshops. Ifeanyi Menkiti, a Nigerian Harvard PhD and Wellesley College professor, was saddened to see the Grolier Bookstore on Plympton Street, founded in 1926, struggling financially, and being a poetry lover, he put it on its feet.

LIBRARIES

What of Harvard and Cambridge has changed least and what most? The paradox can be answered by its libraries. The college took its name from Reverend John Harvard, who came with his wife from England to Charlestown, Massachusetts, in 1637 and died there the next year of consumption at only thirty. In Charlestown, he owned extensive fields for raising cattle and had servants. The parson invited him to assist, and his own house was used as a parsonage sixty years later. Harvard left the newly founded yet unnamed school half his estate (about £800) and his 400 books (329 titles—ancient classics, grammars and Latin, Greek and Hebrew dictionaries), as well as works by Francis Bacon, Desiderius Erasmus and Lorenzo Valla, Latin stylist. Many New Englanders gave small legacies to their church, but John Harvard's bequest was large and suggests that he was keener on learning and his reputation in life than on his place in the afterlife.

Judge Sewall stated in his diary that he spent a night in John Harvard's house in 1697. Presumably, he had a comfortable night. When the college was short of dormitory rooms, Sewall was among the students who had to sleep on a trundle, one or two to a bed. In Sewall's case, he was paired with the Puritan poet Edward Taylor, who stayed his friend. They corresponded from 1674, three years after graduation, until 1729, when Taylor died. (The Sewall surname was changed to Sewell after the family became refugees in London.)

The college's book collection grew to five thousand volumes in the next century and was housed at Harvard Hall. A fire was kept burning at the Hall in the late evening of January 24, 1764. The General Court of Massachusetts had gathered there rather than Boston because of smallpox, and the court decided not to put out the fire so that students returning

Old President's House, 1869 (Wadsworth House). *Cambridge Historical Commission, Charles Sullivan Collection, Harvard Class Album, 1869.*

from vacation might have its benefit. Sparks migrated under the hearth, and the fierce wind of a snowstorm carried them to the wooden beams of the floor below. By the time the flames were noticed in the vacant campus, it was too late to save the Hall. All but 404 of the college's books, some waiting to be shelved and 144 that had been borrowed, were destroyed. The Hall was rebuilt in advance of the Revolution; however, the lead roof of the second iteration, along with certain pewter mugs and plates, was melted down to make bullets.

One surviving book is known to have been given by John Harvard. It is in a case at Houghton Library with the note that John L. Sibley (class of 1825) inserted in it verifying its provenance. On the blank leaf at the beginning of the book are the numbers "3.2.8," for the case, shelf and position, which was the system used at the time the library was burned. The volume's title is *The Christian Warfare Against the Devill World and Flesh: Wherein Is Described Their Nature, the Manner of Their Fight and Meanes to Obtaine Victorye.*

An international call for books ended up with Harvard having an even better collection than before, not only of theology from the attics of the clergy but also books of history, literature and science, as well as scientific instruments. But soon the library was in danger again. Taxation without representation was the object of increased wrath in the colonies, and General Thomas Gage, who replaced Governor Thomas Hutchinson, the last civilian royal governor in 1774, took an aggressive tack in punishing the wayward rebels. Just before the Battle of Bunker Hill, it looked as though Cambridge might become a battlefield; meanwhile, George Washington had requisitioned Harvard's buildings as barracks.

The treasury of reading matter wasn't merely Harvard College's but also the intellectual capital of the Commonwealth. People came in from all over to pack books, load them onto carts and ship them off to Lexington to safety. Some, like Samuel Phillips of Andover, Harvard class of 1771, who supported the revolutionary cause and produced gunpowder for Washington's troops, claimed that they were so occupied in removing the books that they never heard of the siege until it was over. The next June, Harvard reoccupied its buildings.

The clouds of tragedy inhabit the corridors of the great Widener Library, built in 1913. George Widener, a Philadelphia businessman; his wife, Eleanor; and their son, Harry (class of 1907), were traveling home from France in 1912. They had traveled there to choose a chef for Widener's new hotel, the Philadelphia Ritz-Carlton. The Wideners booked their return passage on the *Titanic*. When the ship struck an iceberg, Widener placed his wife and her maid in a lifeboat. They were rescued by a steamship, but George Widener, his valet and Harry perished.

Harry had been a member of the Hasty Pudding Club at Harvard. His passion was books, and to honor him, his mother gave a large donation to the college. No stone, brick or piece of mortar was to be moved or dismantled, lest the library become the property of the City of Cambridge. Bouquets of flowers were to perpetually be placed in the Widener Room on the second floor, which houses Harry's personal book collection. Today, Widener has much of its collection of more than 3 million books off campus, and underground tunnels in the main library require a visitor to take a map or a human guide. Altogether there are at least seventy separate libraries, including the Cabot Science Library, the Islamic Memorial Library of Liturgy and the Schlesinger Library on the history of women in the university system. It is said that late in the twentieth century, these libraries were still communicating by U.S. post and that each library was a byzantine realm of its own. For instance, a student in the Graduate School of Education in 1950 needed a book that the graduate school didn't have. GSE students could use Lamont during summer sessions but no other

Widener Library. *Stephanie Mitchell/Harvard.*

times. She learned that she was the right gender but in the wrong school to use the Radcliffe Library and yet the wrong gender for Widener. So, having obliterated her first name on her library ID card, she put on old jeans and a leather jacket that flattened her chest, stuffed her hair into a wool cap and strode into Lamont for the book.[7]

DINING

Pictures of nineteenth- and early twentieth-century dining show students in Memorial Hall at tables with snowy white tablecloths and formal place settings, while at clubs on special occasions the attire was formal and there were printed menus. The contrast could not have been greater with the early days of Harvard, when the communal table was set with wooden trenchers, steel knives and latten (sheet brass) spoons, wood plates and some stoneware or pewter dishes. Some of the ceramics had initials at the bottom, possibly for their owners, and mugs were shared. Besides porridge and beer, of which there was often a shortage, there was scant meat and oysters, clams and fish. Freshmen—who shoveled snow, picked apples and fed the pigs in Harvard

Yard—were expected to turn the spit and sometimes catch a chicken from a farm and cook it for seniors.

The first student protest in America occurred in 1766, when at the Great Butter Rebellion, Henry Thoreau's grandfather Asa Dunbar stood on a chair and hollered, "Behold our butter stinketh!—give us, therefore, butter that stinketh not."[8] The protest led to a suspension of half of the student body, although the next morning, the student body stood firm and that night dined in town, while Dunbar continued his studies. A food fight that erupted at a Sunday dinner in University Hall on November 1, 1818, saw a furor of coffee, crockery and furniture used as projectiles. On this occasion, the entire sophomore class was expelled.

Documentation from commissary lists and firsthand accounts show why food was the object of such fierce disobedience among students. Essentially, the food was meager, inferior and sometimes rancid. Few students were well off or born gentlemen. Like Cambridge University in England, the college educated future clergy and civil servants. Furthermore, the whole supply chain was Dickensian, with hungry teenagers being the losers. The source of the problems was not the facilities, as the college kitchen was well appointed and had semi-public use by townspeople in the English tradition for large parties. Compared to the domestic economy and cooking on an open fire, the facilities in the original (1682) and second (1764) Harvard Hall were grand. On one hand, the college did not buy forks for student use until 1707; on the other, the kitchen was the most popular catering establishment in the whole countryside. Not only did it supply the commencement dinners and other academic feasts—some of them surprisingly elaborate—but it was also requisitioned (before the local taverns amounted to much) for anything resembling a banquet in the community at large. It provided the entertainment for the Assembly of Elders in 1643 and in 1655 cooked and sent out Tutor Michell's wedding supper.[9]

Nathaniel Eaton, the ill-reputed master of the college before it got the upright Dunster as its first president, had power over dining. Eaton believed that it was his privilege to starve the students. The house and lot given him bordered the Common and may have served as the dormitory where he and his wife lodged and fed the scholars. Before magistrates, Eaton put the blame on his wife for the poor victuals; in her testimony, she said that "the flower [sic] was not so fine as it might, nor so well boiled and stirred"; that "the fish was bad"; that as for beef, they "never had it"; and that her spouse "would call sometimes for butter or cheese when I conceived there was no need of it." The scholars would send down for more meat but were denied what was in the house.[10] As for beverage, the choice was between water and beer, and beer was wanting as much as a week between brewings. Mrs. Eaton did not go so far as to affirm the rumor that the students were given hasty pudding with goat dung in it.

The Eatons fled to Virginia and then returned to England. Some years lapsed until Harvard got the titles back that had been given him; meanwhile, criticisms of Harvard student fare continued. The sharing among all from one vessel of beer, not washed for months, was the status quo. Unwashed knives and forks were carried in the pockets of the scholars' gowns, and napkins were reserved for special occasions and kept with "Commencement Linnen."

Space had been set aside for the commons in the first Harvard building, which burned down, where students and faculty ate together. This nice British custom likely did affect table manners, as an infraction of rudeness at table cost five shillings. In 1790, more than ninety students, or more than half the university, were boarding with private families. Students were forbidden to sup in town, but naturally this was ignored. Judge Paine Wingate (class of 1759) recalled that some of his classmates paid their commons fee but never entered the hall during their collegiate career.

The steward was at first the cook and procurer. This was serious business, as the cost of food was about five times the tuition. Soon the steward's tasks shifted to marketing and accounting. President Dunster, already burdened with finishing the first hall when the building committee left for England, also had to be the steward and direct the brewer, baker, butler and cook.

The style of eating was the English university model of a long dining room table with a screen at the entry, at the other side of which waiters and servants did their work and food was passed up from the buttery (a sort of canteen). The waiters were students, on the model of the University of Cambridge's sizars. This was a sought-after position, as the waiters got the first pick of viands from the kitchen. The punishment for absence from prayers was a penny, but the fine for taking a plum cake was twenty shillings.

Edward Holyoke (class of 1705), who became the tenth Harvard president, enumerated the typical fare of commons: two slices of bread and a quart of beer for breakfast, meat pies at main meals and a pint of milk and half a biscuit for supper. During the American Revolution, tea, coffee and chocolate disappeared from commons, and students had to procure it themselves.

The college could have made things easier had the students all boarded outside the purlieus of the Yard, but the founders believed that the doctrine

J.S. Copley, portrait of Edward Holyoke sitting in the patriarchal Great Chair he acquired for the university, 1773. The building in the background is College Hall and still stands. The view is from Holyoke's residence, Wadsworth House. Gift of Mrs. Turner and Mrs. Ward, granddaughters of Edward Holyoke, 1829. *Harvard Art Museums.*

of predestination was best internalized in commons in a condition of hunger. The obvious attraction of the clubs that were formed after the Revolution was superior dining: the Porcellian was known for its roast pork and the Pudding for great kettles of steaming fare.

It does seem that some self-abnegation was involved—in so many college generations, ill-fed students were throwing foodstuffs, destroying property and setting bonfires in dismay at what was served to commons. It was President Josiah Quincy who reorganized the college curriculum and who made reforms in commons. He had been a graduate in the class of 1790, so he must have had a vivid personal memory when he became president in 1829. To improve the dignity of commons, he imported from England a complete set of table silver embossed with the college seal and a dinner-ware service ornamented with views of college buildings.

Some Harvard students always dined out. In the twentieth century, this might have been a coffee shop, a pizzeria or the Hong Kong in Harvard Square, a tony French restaurant or a graduate student's apartment. Only within the college students tried, as if too hard sometimes, to be primitive. Leverett House used to have parties where the food consisted of champagne and raw oysters. The oysters were shucked by throwing them at the bathroom wall and slurping them straight from the tub.

Progress was made when, long after commons disappeared in 1865, Nathaniel Thayer initiated a low-cost, not-for-profit plan with the motto "Plain food and plenty of it." Students clamored to join. The refectory was supervised by a woman, "Regina Bonarum" or "Queen of the Goodies," and each long table had a waitress. The Thayer meal plan had such success that President Eliot reorganized and expanded it and placed it in the nave of Memorial Hall.

It may be that the problem with institutional food is essentially that it is institutional. A Harvard Law student, Armand, had given over most of his undergraduate time to performing as a concert pianist and in campus theater. Certain of his papers were finished at Hayes-Bickford, the all-night cafeteria that was a twin to Elsie's, both a short walk from the Harvard houses. Armand, like other multitasking students, lamented when "Hayes-Bick" closed between four and five o'clock in the morning in the mid-1960s. What was Harvard coming to? In fact, the City of Cambridge then had a brisk urban feeling day and night, and Harvard Square was understood to be a center of the world.

UNEARTHING HIDDEN HISTORY

The pledge of the college to enroll indigenous Americans resulted in an Indian College built in 1655. Caleb Cheeshahteumuck of the Wampanoag tribe was the first Native American to graduate from Harvard in the class of 1665. Caleb died of tuberculosis in Watertown less than a year after graduation. Another student, Joel Iacoomes, the 1665 class valedictorian, was shipwrecked on his way to commencement from Martha's Vineyard and murdered by robbers. In 2011, he was awarded an honorary bachelor's degree.

The Indian College was torn down in 1698, and Matthews Hall was built on the site. Three centuries later, in 1970, an American Indian Program emerged on campus, and a program was established to address Native American issues. This focuses on interfaculty scholarship, outreach and student recruitment and support.

Harvard's class of 1665 had nine Native American students. One student left after a year to become a seaman, another may have been an ordained minister, one died of smallpox and it is speculated that another was the privy counselor to King Philip (the Wampanoag chief Metacom), whose amicable relations with the colonists turned to armed conflict in 1675. The students seem to have been an elite group who, besides being students, were diplomats for their people.

What was known as the Indian College was a building of four thousand square feet completed in 1656 near where Matthew Hall now stands. Because the first Harvard building (a wooden two-and-a-half-story structure) was falling into disrepair, partly from being built on swamp ground, the indigenous and English students lived in the more sturdily built Indian College.

The printing press also was for some years there. The Indian College's original purpose was twofold. Harvard was close to bankrupt in 1646 and sought financial help in England. The missionary society, called in England the Society for the Propagation of the Gospel, wanted to Christianize the indigenous people. President Dunster sent three Puritans to England to convince the Society that Native Americans needed leaders with a British education. The society agreed with the proviso that there be a new college charter that Indian and English students would be educated together. John Eliot selected two young men to be students. The college promised to waive tuition and provide housing for the students. Native American students went to lectures and dined with the English students. Many would have died of disease consequent to this

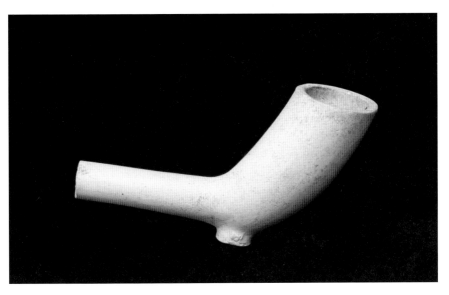

White pipe, a relic from the archaeological dig in Harvard Yard. *Peabody Museum at Harvard.*

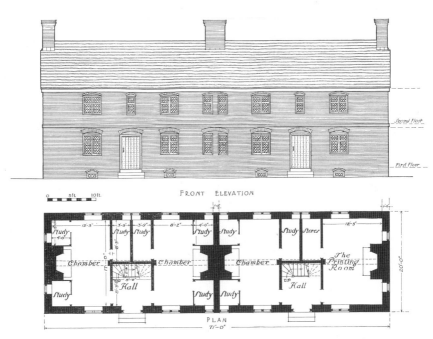

CONJECTURAL RESTORATION OF THE INDIAN COLLEGE, BY H. R. SHURTLEFF, ESQ.

Indian College reconstruction plan. *Harvard University Archives.*

proximity, and the Indian College was not long-lived. Meanwhile, the printing activities thrived.

Besides Native Americans connected to the Indian College, there were translators of the Bible and an assistant printer who laid the type: Wowaus, or James the Printer (an honorary surname). The last Native American student at Harvard in the colonial era was Benjamin Larnell, from Taunton, Massachusetts, who died before graduating with the class of 1716. John Leverett, president of Harvard from 1708 to 1724, in his diary described Larnell as "an Acute Grammarian, an Extraordinary Latin Poet and a good Greek one." Larnell's versification in Latin of Aesop's fable of "The Fox and the Weasel" was discovered in 2012. Poems in Latin, Greek and Hebrew by Larnell were shown off by Samuel Sewell in London.[11] In October 1646, at the Indian settlement of Nonantum, then within Cambridge limits, on the south side of the Charles, Christianizing began and went hand in hand with education.

Part II

BECOMING THE UNITED STATES

TORY ROW

Cambridge was too near to Boston to have significant trade of its own. A traveler of 1750 observed that the town was dependent on the courts and the college. Aristocrats who arrived in that era from plantations in the West Indies were secure in their wealth and status without tilling the soil or sailing their ships. Like the family in Martinique of the future empress Josephine of France, they had means yet lived in fear—of slave revolts, disease and natural disasters. Clustered in stately estates on Brattle Street, which often served merely as summer residences, these slave owning planters would become fugitives in the War for Independence and lose their homes as Harvard and the town turned into barracks and grounds for General Washington's army. Now history condemns these eighteenth-century aristocrats for deriving their wealth from the labor of enslaved people, but such condemnation would have been a distinctly minority view among the residents of Cambridge in those years.

Harvard and Cambridge have a complex set of historical connections to slavery. Andrew Delbanco noted that Harvard "functioned in its own right as a bank by making interest-bearing loans to merchants who used the borrowed capital to finance their slave-trading business."[1]

Three Harvard presidents owned slaves, slaves worked on campus as early as 1639 and among the first residents of Wadsworth House (built in 1726 at the southern edge of Harvard Yard) were the two slaves of President

Broken stone marker on Cambridge Common. *Leon Abdalian, Boston Public Library.*

Benjamin Wadsworth. (A plaque honoring four enslaved persons who once lived in Wadsworth House was affixed there by the university in 2016.) Slave labor, of course, also underwrote the success of Harvard's early benefactors until the Civil War; they lived in affluent ease, and unlike for the Puritans there was "mixt" dancing at their parties.

Dr. Catlin Hopkins commented, "During the middle of the 18th century, every person in a position of authority at Harvard was a slave owner—the president, the professors, the head tutor. Working for Harvard meant that they didn't have to pay taxes on the people they enslaved. It was subsidized slave ownership."[2]

"Your lot buys it, my lot inherits it," said the Earl's daughter Mary to her plutocrat suitor in *Downton Abbey*, and the wealth from the sugar plantations would have seemed an eternal benefit of their lifestyle to Colonel Brattle and, of his nine children, the two, Thomas and Elizabeth, who survived.

The splendid eighteenth-century domestic architecture of Brattle Street in Cambridge reflects the power of those who built these homes but not the unsavory means that created it. In the Revolutionary era, Brattle Street curved along the Charles River from the center of Cambridge, and each grand house had substantial land and a patrician presence.

The street itself takes its name from Major General William Brattle, Harvard class of 1722, a clergyman, physician and lawyer who first sided with the Patriots but subsequently became a military officer for the Crown. When he built his house on the street that was to bear his name, he was the richest person in the Massachusetts Bay Colony. Brattle secretly informed on rebel activity in Cambridge. He told General Gage about the steady removal of gunpowder by the Patriots to Castle William in Boston Harbor.

Brattle was shot at as he fled to Boston across the Brighton Bridge in the summer of 1774. He left for Halifax with the British military, dying there seven months later at seventy. It seems that Brattle left all his property in Cambridge to his only surviving son Thomas, Harvard class of 1760. Thomas raised aquatic plants, had a goldfish pond and apparently helped create a bath for Harvard

John Vassall's silver tankard by Joseph Kneeland (1698/99–1740). Gift from John Vassall, class of 1732. *Harvard Art Museum.*

students at a spot known as "Brickwharf" near what is now Memorial Drive. In the past, a Bath Lane Marker explained that there were in 1781 medicated vapor baths for ladies and gentlemen, as well as a large open swimming bath where young gentlemen learned to swim. This college bath on the Charles was paid for by fundraising and subscription (detailed records are preserved in the Harvard archives).

Son Thomas was sympathetic to the demands of the colonies, although he associated with Loyalists in England. He sailed to England, declared himself a neutral and is said to have alleviated the plight of American prisoners during the Revolution. As Thomas Brattle convinced the government that he had supported the rebels in the war, unlike most of the proprietors of homes on Tory Row, he and his sister retained their property. When Thomas returned to America, however, he lived in Rhode Island.

Immediately to the west of the Brattle House is the house of Colonel Henry Vassall. Henry Vassall spent a great deal of money gambling and managed to run out of nearly all his property. When dying, he asked his servants to pray for him. They answered that he might pray for himself.

Henry was forty-eight when he died in 1769. His widow, Penelope, a daughter of Isaac Royall, left in 1774 for Antigua, where her father owned a sugar plantation, and eventually settled in London. Isaac Royall had seven sons, all of whom were slave owners. By the end of 1775, most of the interrelated residents of Brattle Street had departed and left their furnishings behind, knowing that they were unwelcome to the Patriots. The house was seized by the Patriots and became the quarters of the medical department of the Continental army. Penelope returned to Boston from London but never regained her status or money. The Henry Vassall house was heavily mortgaged, with those mortgages later foreclosed by one John Pitt.

Hundreds of enslaved people worked on the Vassalls' plantations in Jamaica. Slaves also worked in their elegant homes (one of which later became the Longfellow House), set back on a slope overlooking the Charles. Thomas Vassall on the eve of Revolution had eleven house slaves. It was after the Battle of Bunker Hill that the house was lent by its new owner (sympathetic to the Rebel cause) to the Patriots for use as a hospital.

One enslaved couple who lived on Tory Row were Anthony (Tony), a coachman, and his wife, Cuba. First owned by John Vassall's uncle Henry, at Henry's death Tony was kept by Vassall's wife, Penelope, at 94 Brattle. Penelope sold Cuba and their children across Brattle Street to John Vassall, trying to pay Henry's debts. This was 105 Brattle, perhaps the grandest

Penelope Royall Vassall, born in Antigua in 1723, died in Boston in 1800. Portrait by Joseph Blackburn. *Massachusetts Historical Society.*

mansion of Tory Row. The enslaved couple spent almost sixty years in slavery. They were legally property even after the Vassalls fled. Anthony and Cuba continued to live east of the garden on a portion of the John Vassall estate after they had their freedom. Tony acquired a small house and worked as a farrier. He and his wife successfully petitioned to keep their house, and the grant of their small pension signed by Governor John Hancock is at the Houghton Library. Their son Darban was active in the civil rights community in Boston. He and his brother Cyrus were founding members of the African Society in 1796, and Darby toasted at a banquet celebrating the anniversary of Haitian independence.

The farthest of the estates from Harvard Square was built for Lieutenant Governor Thomas Oliver, sworn in less than a month before most of his wealthy neighbors were driven behind British army lines. Oliver was the grandson of Isaac Royall. One of the Fireside Poets, James Russell Lowell (class of 1838), was born in 1819 in the house and later named it Elmwood. Lowell wrote, "My Elmwood chimneys seem crooning to me, /As of old in their moody, minor key." His friend Longfellow wrote a poem about his house too, of which a single stanza shows a stirring mood, heartening in the post–Civil War period:

Sing of the air, and the wild delight
Of wings that uplift and winds that uphold you,
The joy of freedom, the rapture of flight
Through the drift of the floating mists that enfold you.

Elmwood is a discreet residence. Like many of the historic houses on Brattle Street, Elmwood is sometimes referred to by a hyphenated name that highlights its successive owners, being known as the Oliver-Gerry-Lowell House. Derek Bok chose to move to Elmwood from the traditional home of university presidents across from the Yard on Quincy Street because of construction work going on around it, as well as the unrest of students. Adjacent to Elmwood is Lowell Park, a state-owned park that was part of the original Oliver estate. A list at Elmwood tells the roles of Cambridge slaves there, such as footman, gardener or seamstress. One enslaved artisan, "Buff," was a blacksmith who was hired out to Jonathan Sewall. Having settled in St. John, New Brunswick, the younger Sewall found a position in the law and devoted much time to cultivating his garden, whose seeds often came from back home in Massachusetts.

The last attorney general of the colony, Jonathan Sewall, was a close friend to John Adams, who graduated with him in the Harvard class of 1754. Sewall was also the brother-in-law of John Hancock. Friends of the Loyalists piled furnishings inside Sewall's Brattle Street house to barricade the entrance, nailed down the doors and set up guards, but mobs broke in and plundered the house. They also marched on Harvard Square and made two Loyalist judges sign papers of resignation.

Number 175 Brattle Street was built in about 1764 by a West Indies plantation owner, George Ruggles, whose wife, Susanna, was the sister of Henry Vassall. George owned Caribbean plantations, and his fine house on Brattle Street had forty acres. Ruggles escaped to England before the outbreak of the Revolution, selling his estate to Thomas Fayerweather. The summer after the Battle of Bunker Hill, the house was used as a hospital, but after the British evacuated in March 1776, the Fayerweathers reclaimed their property.

Many buildings dating back to the pre-Revolutionary period survive as private homes or historic houses open to the public. The Cooper-Frost-Austen House on Linnean Street (1681) is preserved very much as it was, whereas the Hooper-Lee-Nichols House on Brattle Street (1685) has been much remodeled and is the headquarters of the Cambridge Historical Society. The William Brattle House at 42 Brattle Street (1727) is owned and maintained by the Cambridge Center for Adult Education, which also owns the historic Dexter Pratt House, where the blacksmith of Longfellow's famous poem lived.

PROFESSOR WINTHROP

Governor Winthrop's great-great-grandson, also named John Winthrop, graduated at eighteen in Harvard's class of 1732. This John Winthrop, like many other Enlightenment scientists, had catholic interests—in astronomy, meteorology, mathematics and geology. He also served as president of Harvard for one year. John Adams recommended Professor Winthrop to George Washington as one of the local men whose judgment could be most relied on.

Winthrop's core fields were physics and astronomy. He held the chair at Harvard of Hollis Professor of Mathematics and Natural Philosophy; Thomas Hollis was a wealthy London merchant who gave this first endowed professorship in North America to Harvard in 1721.

In the day, the study of astronomy in particular was led by enthusiasts and scarcely professionalized. Ministers were computing eclipses and observing the stars.

Harvard's President Edward Holyoke performed electrical experiments with Winthrop. Winthrop used recycled materials to assemble his globe electricity-producing machine, including an egg cup, broken goblet and cookie press.

Winthrop taught on location. He took students to the North Shore to see a comet pass. He took them to the top of a Harvard building to look through his shiny brass telescope. John Adams chose his favorite professor well.

Painting of Professor Winthrop. He holds a diagram showing the Transit of Venus. He gave it to the college in 1779. *Collection of Historical Scientific Instruments.*

There were intellectual societies in colonial times. Yet Benjamin Thompson and Loammi Baldwin, an inventor/politician and an engineer, respectively, both from Woburn, Massachusetts, were a society of two, plain folk who fashioned for themselves a higher education.

Loammi worked with his family of engineers and grew up to oversee the building of the Middlesex Canal. Benjamin, apprenticed to a grocer near

Faneuil Hall, used to drop under the counter to do science and study French. He was a Loyalist and spy for the Crown. He and Benjamin Franklin, born some years before in another Massachusetts town, were equally famous in Europe for their science and philosophy in their day.

After two years as an apprentice, Benjamin returned to home and studied medicine with a doctor in Woburn. In his diary, he described his free time as from five to bedtime, when he would "follow what my inclination leads me to; whether it be to go abroad, or stay at home and read either Anatomy, Physic, or Chemistry, or any book I want to Peruse."[3]

What sparked their dedication to science and invention was first the inspiration of Franklin, whose kite and key experiment to conduct electricity they copied, getting singed, and secondly that of Professor Winthrop of Harvard. All the month of June 1770, Benjamin and Loammi, both teenagers, walked ten miles to Cambridge and back to attend the natural philosophy lectures at Harvard given by Winthrop, its star professor.

Winthrop became the first chaired professor in America after being examined on religious matters to rule out heresy. A setback in scientific work occurred when Harvard Hall burned down in 1764 (the court, which had convened there, left embers burning after a meeting as a courtesy to the students the next morning). However, gifts of scientific instruments in the wake of the loss rebuilt the scientific instrument collection. Winthrop used a twenty-four-foot telescope from Hollis and one that had belonged to Edmond Halley, on whose Halley's Comet Winthrop lectured at Harvard in 1682. Franklin gave Harvard a machine that sparked electricity.

Winthrop's chair of natural philosophy was the rubric for many lines of study of the rationalist Enlightenment, as opposed to religion, the classics, mathematics or languages. It included science from chemistry and physics to mechanics, meteorology and biology. Benjamin and Loammi must have looked at the satellites of Jupiter when they gazed through the twenty-eight-foot refractory telescope from the roof at Harvard Hall. This was the type and the same approximate size as the telescope Christiaan Huyghens invented and through which he was able to describe the rings of Saturn. Winthrop's lectures were a breath of fresh air, and as usual, Benjamin and Loammi must have talked science most of the walk.

As impressive as the enthusiasm of the two farm boys from Woburn is that Harvard opened the lectures of this most eminent professor to those from the surrounding towns not pursuing a degree (instead of marginalizing them). This paved the way for Harvard and Cambridge to be an intellectual center in years to come. This was the time when Harvard trained ministers and the lists of students were published by prominence; to apply on merit would have been preposterous. Winthrop taught science supported by many microscopes, telescopes and the like. Although not slated for an advanced formal education, Thompson and Baldwin were fascinated, and his intellect caught fire from Winthrop. Baldwin became a pioneering civil engineer, and Benjamin became an outstanding inventor in Europe.

The kite in a storm represented an early form of empirical research, working out answers in the field. Loammi would recall feeling dazed and weak limbed, and he appeared to spectators in a bright flame as he brought flashing lights of static electricity to his conductor during a storm.

Consequent to the importance to the faithful of the star that guided the Wise Men to Jesus, early scientific research in America included the astronomical, and the colony and the college shared in stargazing expeditions. Many European observatories and the Philadelphia society cooperated in these missions, and in Philadelphia David Rittenhouse prepared to observe the transit of Venus over the disc of the sun. A special act of government granted use of the Provincial sloop to convey Winthrop and two assistants, with instruments loaned by the college, to St. John's, Newfoundland, to compute the transit of Venus (June 3, 1769). Newfoundland was the only British colony in which an observation of the phenomenon could be made, being the westernmost part of the earth where the end of the transit could be seen, as the phenomenon was to happen before the sun would rise in any other part of America except the coast of Labrador.

Professor Winthrop made similar observations in Cambridge. Due to ill health, he was not able to journey to Lake Superior to see the beginning and end of the transit. He died in the spring of 1779 and left his telescope to Harvard. In appreciation for his inspiring teacher, Benjamin Thompson, who began life as a fatherless farm boy and became Count Rumford of the Holy Roman Empire, endowed the Rumford chair at Harvard.

GENERAL AND MRS. WASHINGTON

Martha Washington had never been farther north than Alexandria, Virginia, when she set out for the winter headquarters of her husband, during the Siege of Boston (1775). The general sent the aide-de-camp Colonel George Baylor to Connecticut to meet her. Washington arrived in Cambridge on July 2. Samuel Langdon, president of Harvard, welcomed him as a guest in his house. Langdon's sympathies were with the rebels, but for religious reasons. He was a strict Congregationalist who feared that Britain would impose the Anglican faith on the American colonies.

On July 3, General Washington inspected the troops. Forty-two drummers and fifers led the troops through town, and at Cambridge common he drew his sword and formally took command. Everyone wanted to see Washington, as subjects of royalty would wish to touch their king, and everyone was impressed. Washington was less impressed, finding the conditions deplorable, although he observed that the men would fight well if properly officered.[4] He was still staying at the president's house when Abigail Adams wrote to her husband on July 16 that the general made an even more favorable impression by half than her husband had prepared her for: "Dignity with ease, and complacency, the Gentleman and soldier look agreeably blended in him. Modesty marks every line and feture of his face."[5]

He was forty-three and, so far, had only led a few hundred men. The camp in Cambridge was a disorganized scene, and the soldiers were not the spit and polish he was accustomed to. The day after the inspection, Colonel Glover's regiment of fishermen from Marblehead arrived in baggy pants and their clothes tarred, as that kept them resistant to water at sea. But Washington got them drilling, made improvements to the camp and began to reconcile the militias from the different colonies. The Marlboro regiment of North Shore fishermen would row George Washington across the Delaware River to march to Trenton. The house of the president of Harvard College wouldn't do as a headquarters. The house was too close to the British for comfort, a half mile closer to the Charles Bridge in Boston, and there was a fear of a push back from besieged Boston. He may have chafed at being someone's guest, and his soldiers were all around, 1,520 housed in three Harvard buildings by January, while others stayed in taverns and the houses of Patriots.

After a short visit at the president's house, Washington moved with his staff to a more spacious headquarters, the largest and most elegant house in Cambridge, from which Loyalist John Vassall had recently fled for Boston, remaining until the British military evacuated them in March to Nova Scotia. Responding to the Lexington alarm, when the British were on their way to foil the minutemen, Captain Benedict Arnold arrived with the Connecticut Footguards. They stayed at the mansion owned by Lieutenant Governor Oliver. Initially, most of the soldiers did not take up the empty Loyalist houses. The Battle of Bunker Hill prompted more regiments ordered to Cambridge. Many camped in churches and taverns, as well as on the estate

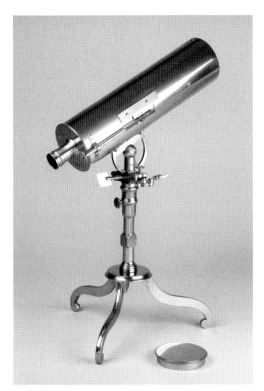

Left: Cassegrain reflecting telescope by James Short, circa 1758. This folded two-mirror design was named after its inventor, Laurent Cassegrain, a seventeenth-century French priest from the Chartres region. *Collection of Historical Scientific Instruments, Putnam Gallery of Harvard. President and Fellows of Harvard College.*

Below: "Washington taking command of the American Army at Cambridge, July 3, 1775."

of Ralph Inman east of the town center; General Putnam took over the Inman house as his headquarters, though as a gallant officer sent a guard with Elizabeth Inman when she visited her husband in Boston. By the time Washington left for New York in March, New England troops had filled the Loyalist houses to the brim. There is a story of Thomas Fayerweather, a plantation owner, coming home from a trip to his house at 175 Brattle and finding a regiment quartered in his mansion. Several hundred soldiers were living in a single Cambridge house that winter, and complaints were of no blankets, soap or beer. Most of the splendid mansions west of the Cambridge town center were occupied, no longer by interrelated carefree country gentlefolk who assembled every afternoon in one or another of their houses but by soldiers with the mission of corralling the British in Boston and Charlestown.

An evocative description of accommodations at the former Vassall House comes from Patricia Brady's *Martha Washington: An American Life*:

> *Being the commander's wife was something like being a fraternity house mother. Martha and George were in their mid-forties, living with a large group of men in their twenties—Washington's aides-de-camp and a shifting number of other bachelor officers and visitors. The young men slept two or three to a bed and several to a room; they were always bustling back and forth on military errands, sometimes seeking out their own private entertainments of the sort not best shared with Lady Washington.*[6]

The provincial authorities assigned two local farmers, brothers Joseph and Parsons Smith, to look after the Vassall property. Grass from hayfields on the property of Tories, after they left, was given to local Patriot farmers. Much went to fodder the horses of the army. Washington refused a salary, but his barns were always filled.

Washington wanted Martha to join him. He was concerned that Mount Vernon might be a target, whereas the general's Cambridge headquarters were secure behind the lines, and eighteenth-century armies usually sat out the winter season. Martha had also heard that summer the gossip about her husband having an affair with a washerwoman. Martha traveled with her son Jacky; his wife, Nelly; a maid; and a coachman in scarlet livery the five hundred miles to Cambridge in stages. As they passed, people in the towns cheered, and newspapers treated her arrival like society news.

Martha left Mount Vernon mid-November and arrived in Cambridge nearly one month later. She wrote to her friend Elizabeth Ramsay:

*I now sit down to tell you that I arrived hear safe and our party all well—
we were fortunate in our time of setting out as the weather proved fine all
the time we were on the road—I did not reach Philad till the Tuesday after
I left home, we were so attended and the gentlemen so kind, that I am under
obligations to them that I shal not for get soon. I don't doubt but you have
see the Figures our arrive made in the Philadelpha paper—and I left it in
as great pomp as if I had been a very great somebody.*

    *I have waited some days to collect something to tell, but ailas there is
nothing but what you will find in the papers—every person seems to be
cheerfull and happy hear—some days we have a number of cannon and
shells from Boston and Bunkers Hill, but it does not seem to surprise any
one but me;—I confess I shudder every time I hear the sound of a gun—. I
have been to dinner with two of the Generals, Lee and Putnam, and I just
took a look at pore Boston & Charlestown from prospect Hill Charlestown
has only a few chimneys standing in it, there seems to be a number of very
fine Buildings in Boston but god knows how long they will stand; they are
pulling up all the warfs for firewood—to me that never see any thing of
war, the preparations, are very terable indeed, but I endever to keep my fears
to myself as well as I can.*[7]

Martha settled into the three-story Georgian mansion that John Vassall
had built in 1759 when he was still a teenager. General Lee stayed in a
different house. Eventually, part of it was a hospital. She entertained many
people who wanted to visit with Washington—members of Congress,
Massachusetts officials and Revolutionary leaders like John Adams and Ben
Franklin, as well as the officers. The general met with them in his office,
which was also the dining room off the front hall. Martha took over the
reception room as her parlor. Martha's outgoing nature served her well. She
greeted visitors with tea, oranges and conversation and hosted dinner parties
for the young officers. The wife of Reverend Dr. Samuel Cooper, pastor of
the Brattle Street Church, preferred to dine elsewhere, with her relatives.
The reason seems to have been that the talk was all military: Washington
regularly wanted to have at his table the field officer of the day, the adjutant
of the day and other army officers and political notables. There was criticism
in Philadelphia of a plan for a ball to honor Martha; it was dropped, but she
persisted in her efforts to socialize, with modest entertainments in Cambridge
attended by important figures, including Abigail Adams and generals and
other officers. Not everybody had the civility of the Virginians—an inebriated
Major General Charles Lee introduced Abigail to his dogs at dinner.

Martha arrived at a low point. Many soldiers had returned to their farms, and supplies were sparse. She asked that Christ Church, Cambridge, be readied for a prayer service and asked for the customary prayer for the king to be taken out. Repairs were made to please her. At Christmas, Martha was as serene as ever at church and wished people the compliments of the season.

This church had been close by to the wealthy residents of Brattle Street. Benjamin Franklin's grave is in the northwest corner of its burying ground, which was also a sheep pasture until 1702.

The church also provided Anglican services to students at Harvard College across the Cambridge Common. It was built on a granite foundation formed of ballast stones of ships that came into Boston Harbor; originally, the exterior was finished in sanded paint to look like an English stone church. For Washington's army, Christ Church was barracks for the Connecticut troops, and the Common was used for a mustering ground—church windows were broken, so it must have been very cold. At a funeral held for a young British officer, a mob heavily damaged the church after the service. Services were continued there again from 1790.

Many new recruits came to the camp, and strategy and organization became more urgent. Washington, joined by John Adams, met on January 16, 1776, with his council of war/generals. The objective, as stated by Congress in Philadelphia, was no longer to reestablish harmony with Britain but to destroy the army and navy at Boston even if this meant burning the town. The first major offensive of the Continental forces occurred outside the British-occupied city of Quebec during a snowstorm, ending with the commander of the offensive, Benedict Arnold, wounded. Two months later, while the Americans held their fire, the British evacuated Boston. Their troops and supporters were rowed out to be packed into warships to regroup in Nova Scotia, and the first stage of the Revolution was over. A new flag was raised by the Americans on the first of January.

Did General Washington take command of the army under the elm where a granite monument was placed in 1864? Documentation is scarce. Tradition has it that Martha gave a Twelfth Night party on Epiphany, which was also the occasion of the Washingtons' seventeenth wedding anniversary; George Washington likely frowned at the idea of a party as frivolous, especially in Puritan Boston and in a time of war, but became persuaded that "a little amusement often served to raise the spirits of both officers and men."[8]

The oldest source is an 1855 biography of Washington by Washington Irving that notes that Mrs. Washington "claimed to keep twelfth-night in due style." No contemporary letter, diary entry or newspaper from 1776 describes such a party, although scholars have noted that at least once, on January 6, 1773, Mount Vernon had more guests than usual. A U.S. Department of Interior report supposed there may have been such a party and, later, that the Longfellows celebrated Twelfth Night themselves. In 1900, Alice M. Longfellow said in the *Cambridge Tribune* that Washington rarely "allowed any merriment at headquarters or took any part in revelry himself"; after Martha arrived, "she and her husband celebrated their wedding anniversary, though the General had to be much persuaded by his aides."[9]

A Great Cake was a common dessert in the colonial period, and it is a firm fact that Martha had her servants bake it for her parties. The recipe used flour, butter and sugar, currants, nutmegs, cloves, cinnamon, mace and caraway seeds. It is noted by the archives at Mount Vernon that the foam that rises to the top of fermented liquor (the barm) was used for leavening; liquid derived from posset, a mixture of warm ale and cream, was added, and the cake was baked at a high temperature. That was reduced once the cake started to rise and firm. The recipe, written out by Martha's granddaughter Martha Parke Custis, suggested slightly different ingredients as well as forty eggs, wine and brandy. Fruitcake-like eggnog was a grownup dessert. This was passed on down through generations of Martha's family. This was the cake served at the Christmas festivities in 1797 after George Washington declined to serve a third term as president and made his farewell to politics.

Martha eased the life of the general by her caring presence. Washington knew that he was neglectful of points of etiquette, given his distraction to other matters, whereas Martha had a way of smoothing things over in trying circumstances. She was a refined hostess at entertainments, where punch was poured freely, and there would have been music and reels.

On April 4, the general left. Martha and the Custises two days before, despite the outbreak of smallpox in Boston, dined there as guests of a prominent merchant, John Andrews, an eyewitness to the Boston Tea Party. George and Martha traveled south separately, he on horseback and she and the Custises by coach. Martha moved into the general's new headquarters in New York, while the Custises continued home to Virginia. George Washington was in Cambridge again as president-elect in 1789.

For a half century after the American army lodged in Cambridge during the winter of 1775–76, there was a scarcity of fuel wood. Firewood came from the seven thousand acres that Harvard owned east of the Penobscot Bay in Maine.

CHRISTMAS AT 149 BRATTLE STREET

The Christmas tree is thought by some to have originated with Martin Luther, who saw the starry night and wanted to bring its splendor inside for his family. The evergreen decorated with candles, fruits and berries was called a *Tannenbaum* and was familiar to the Alsatians by 1600.

Just when the custom of trimming a tree as the centerpiece of Christmas festivities in the home came to North America can be conjectured with fair likelihood and involves a congenial baroness during the War for Independence.

Frederika Charlotte Riedesel was the daughter of a minister at the Prussian court. Her husband, Friederich Adolphus Riedesel, was a baron and army officer in

Engraving of Baroness Fredericka Riesdesel. *Bridgeman Images, no date.*

service to the Duke of Brunswick. In the Seven Years' War, Baron Riedesel was wounded, and sixteen-year-old Charlotte nursed him back to health. In the mid-1770s, King George III of England needed to quiet the American colonists, but he didn't want to have English fighting English. He made an agreement with the Duke of Brunswick to send four thousand German soldiers to America to fight the rebel colonists, and Von Riedesel was promoted to general and put in command of the first dispatch of soldiers.

Lady Riedesel would not be left behind. She was pregnant when her husband traveled across the Atlantic (they had nine children, six of whom survived to adulthood), but as soon as she recovered, she had a commodious carriage built and crossed Europe with two daughters, soon sailing to Canada. She and her husband were reunited before the Battle at Saratoga.

The year she arrived, 1777, was a tumultuous one in the war. A British force captured Fort Ticonderoga but was driven from Canada and surrendered on October 17, 1777, at Saratoga. The prisoners, British and German, were marched from Saratoga to Albany and on to Boston. By the terms of surrender made by General Burgoyne to General Gates, the English and German soldiers were not officially prisoners of war but rather "troops of the Convention," which put the Riedesels in an equivocal (but better off) state during their captivity. Cambridge became a detention camp for Burgoyne's army, with homes that the Royalists had quit serving among the barracks.

The six years that Lady Riedesel spent in Canada and America testify to how war differed for high-ranking officers. Her diary tells of near misses, tending to the wounded and reprimanding generals when the troops were at starvation point. The baroness wore men's boots, and a shoemaker in charge of the Americans kept the officers' and her footwear in repair. General Schuyler became a friend during a three-day stop in Albany, and later in Europe, General Riedesel asked after him. Lady Riedesel met Lafayette in Hartford and invited him to dinner; they spoke French, to the Americans' dismay.

People were being tarred and feathered and guns were fired near at hand, but nothing conveys the privilege and politeness as well as where the baroness and her children were billeted after being in the attic of a farmhouse (near Winter Hill in Somerville) when they first arrived in Boston. Her rare complaint was that the farmer's wife extracted lice from her daughter's head at the dining table. Three weeks later, they were taken to Cambridge and put up in one of the Royalists' properties on Tory Row. There would have been few Tories left on Brattle Street, but she recalled hearing of afternoon parties with music and dancing at one or another house:

> *The owners gathered every afternoon at one of the homes or another, where they enjoyed themselves with music and dancing, living happily in comfort and harmony until, alas, the devastating war separated them all, leaving all the houses desolate with the exception of two, whose owners shortly thereafter were also obliged to flee.*[10]

The baroness was warm, pretty, kind and popular. In Cambridge, while her husband was in Boston, and later, on the British side, with her husband, in Quebec, she was all vigor and in excellent spirits. She liked Cambridge so much that she felt reluctant to depart.

Now called the Lechmere-Sewall-Riedesel House, the residence dates from 1760. It was built by Richard Lechmere on land inherited by Mary Phipps, his wife. Mary was the daughter of William Phipps, a shepherd in (now) Woolrich, Maine, until age eighteen, who in his thirties recovered a large treasure from a sunken Spanish galleon and later became governor of Massachusetts as "Sir Phipps." He built a grand mansion on what is now Otis Street in East Cambridge and invited his friends to a housewarming that included a husking frolic—presumably entertainment akin to a hayride.

Sadly, the house caught fire and, before the next party, had burned to the ground. Lechmere needed to cover his debts, so he sold the property to Jonathan Sewall in the early 1770s. In 1774, a mob swarmed the house and forced Sewall to resign his office of attorney general.

While residing at 149 Brattle Street, the baroness scratched her name into a windowpane on the north side of the house—it is still visible. Despite what some accounts suggest, the occupancy by Lady Riedesel lasted from October or November 1777 to November 1778, when she was escorted to Virginia. The dates are pertinent, as on Christmas 1777 she was in the beautiful Georgian home that it was her responsibility to furnish. Very likely this lighthearted hostess and mother arranged for a *Tannenbaum* for her parlor in the home that met her needs as well.

The Riedesels received orders to depart to Virginia, and Lady Riedesel became friends with Martha Wayles Jefferson. On the third anniversary of independence (July 4, 1779), Jefferson had been elected governor of Virginia and was about to assume office. He wrote an ardent letter to Von Riedesel that day (one can hardly believe it was wartime). The general and his wife had been an important part of the Jeffersons' society, and Thomas Jefferson conveyed that his wife, Martha, particularly missed her German friend and that the "commission as to the spoons" would be brought by Jefferson to her.

Before their return to Germany in 1783, the Riedesels spent a pleasant interlude in Quebec. Officially, the general was leading the Brunswick (German) regiment to protect Canada from attacks by Americans. They lived in a residence given them by the government of the newly established colony of Canada, in Sorel, twenty-five miles northeast of Montreal, on the south bank of the St. Lawrence River. The house would become the Maison des Gouverneurs because several governors of Quebec starting with Sir Guy Carleton summered there. This small town recalls the baroness's gardens, the four hundred apple trees she had planted there, her parties and the Christmas tree. In the German tradition, the tree is selected in the fall. The children are not to see it until it is decorated, which was likely the tradition of the Riedesels wherever they lived.

Were the grounds of the Lechemere-Sewall-Riedesel house excavated, vestiges might be found such as have been found since 2021 on the Maison des Gouverneurs property—small kegs for rum, phials for grappa, port and sherry bottles and tableware, including whole services of the fine white creamware that the baroness would have carried with her on her journeys. After the fanciest banquet, dishware might have been tossed out rather than washed, in order to enhance the impression of opulence.

Among others credited with bringing the tradition of decorating Christmas trees to America is the estimable Karl Charles Follen, Harvard's first professor of German. Harvard expelled Professor Follen for his outspoken antislavery views in 1835. The next year, Henry Longfellow replaced Follen as the Smith Professor of Modern Languages. The two became close friends. Follen designed the lovely octagonal sanctuary of the Unitarian-Universalist Church located in his church in East Lexington, where my son's family worships today.

Student Life

Early on, Harvard College had parietals and discipline like the colleges at Cambridge and Oxford in England, where discipline had tightened by 1600. This passage from Hastings Rashdall's *The University of Europe in the Middle Ages* could as well have described sixteenth-century Harvard:

> *The statutes became increasingly minute and restrictive in their interference with all manner of "unacademic" pleasures, in the strictness with which they require attendance at university and college exercises, including the hall dinner with the post-prandial disputations. A visit to the tavern or even the kitchen of the college or hall, becomes a university offence.*[11]

According to Rashdall, discipline of an English university college and in turn Harvard before the 1700s was little different from that of a grammar school. For instance, the college barbers enforced close-cropped hair. A striking incident occurred at Trinity College, Cambridge University, when the president seized a long-haired student in the buttery and chopped off his hair with a bread knife. Yet the little Harvard College of the1600s was positioned by the Puritans for future international renown. The settlers of Cambridge expected that worthies in England would send their sons across the ocean for a more orthodox college experience (e.g., longer days of prayerfulness and fewer distractions), contrasting to what they could get at Oxford or Cambridge. In those early days, a fair number of students were drawn from Britain with no middle stop as New Englanders. Some were like overwrought children known to make a ruckus. At the first commencement of 1644, some of these boys robbed two homes and stole money. Commencement was a traditional time for pandemonium for town and gown; moreover, window breaking, according to Samuel Eliot Morison,

Battle in Common Hall, 1819. *Harvard University Libraries.*

was a frequent means by which the student body of ministers' and upwardly mobile yeomen's sons of Harvard let off steam. Writing of conflicts between clerks and laymen that persisted in the seventeenth century, Morison noted, "In January 1658/59 (so President Chauncy deposed) there was a great disorder at Cambridge…and fighting between the schollars and some of the towne."[12]

No young scholar could be admitted to the early Harvard who could not understand Tully (Cicero) or other Classical writers, and students had to speak true Latin in verse and prose. The nine young men who graduated in the class of 1641 had to read the Bible twice a day, not go abroad to other towns without permission and never voice a profanity. Meanwhile, the college was short of funds, and the stewards' bills were paid with meat, grain, butter, cheese, cider, candles and sometimes tobacco.

In about 1700, Increase Mather burned a book in the college yard. Cotton Mather, Increase's son, opined in print that witchcraft was an evil magical power bent on overturning the Puritan colony. It was a book that refuted this, Robert Calef's *Wonders of the Invisible World*, that Increase cast into the flames to shield his son from ridicule or opprobrium.

Regarding student life at Harvard, 1800 seems to have been an approximate divide. Of course, there was no more punishment for speaking in one's mother tongue.

Timothy Fuller (Harvard class of 1801) was a resident of Cambridge from 1802 to 1833, a politician and a lawyer in Boston. A distinguished orator, he made speeches against relocating the Seminole Indians and against admitting Missouri as a slave state (the Missouri Compromise). Fuller was an ardent supporter of John Quincy Adams and published a widely circulated pamphlet titled "The Election for the Presidency Considered." He kept a diary as a student and young man about town in Cambridge:

We avoided a lesson in Homer by pretending to have received wrong information concerning the exercises of the ensuing week. (August 27, 1798)

Took coffee at Pillsbury's room with Abbot, Allen, Cummings, Dawes, Phinney, Peirce, and Pillsbury. The object is to form a social club of the most respectable characters in the class, whose sentiments on most important subjects will be generally uniform; not demagogues—fishers for popularity—but such as will act on liberal principles uninfluenced by temporary applause or disapprobation. (August 28, 1798)

President Washington's birthday kept on as a fast throughout the Union. In the evening the Hasty Pudding Club met at Cummings' room and according to appointment I spoke on "The Influence of Example." We then went in procession to Porter's and with the seniors took a decent repast and drank sixteen patriotic toasts; eleven of these were written by myself. My oration met with undeserved indulgence and approbation. (February 22, 1801)[13]

The following day, despite the sixteen toasts at Porter's Hotel, Timothy walked to Boston and attended church, where he saw two pretty girls, the Misses Swan. In the afternoon, Timothy went to hear Emerson at the old brick meetinghouse.[14]

Being respected was essential to intellectual development and happiness. Overall, the atmosphere was what William Wordsworth experienced at the University of Cambridge in his studies, where "many books/ Were skimmed, devoured, or studiously perused, / But with no settled plan. I was detached/ Internally from academic cares."[15] Regarding student life, Wordsworth also nostalgically wrote, in *The Prelude* (Book 3):

> *Companionships,*
> *Friendships, acquaintances, were welcomed all*
> *We sauntered, played, or rioted; we talked*
> *Unprofitable talk at morning hours;*
> *Drifted about along the streets and walks,*
> *Read lazily in trivial books, went forth*
> *To gallop through the country in blind zeal.*

Some remember the all-nighters, whereas other returning graduates have had the perspective that the student body was working all the time, not like the fun old days. The very existence of hazing is like a house of mirrors.

A seventeenth-century student who had wealth gave £100 before entering the freshman class, plus double tuition and a silver plate during his first year. This gave him the privilege of sitting at the head table with the faculty (better and hotter food) and exemption from running messages for seniors, a practice at Oxford and Cambridge carried over from England. In exchange for a silver tankard, the privileges of high class made a student exempt from discipline, let him wear a special hat and have the title of "Master." Fellow Commoners were those of a superior caste, linked in the first Harvard College laws of 1642 to 1746 with being "a Knights Eldest Sonne or of Superior Nobility." The boys could drink from their tankards while at the college but had to leave them behind after graduating as college property. The tankards given by two brothers, John and William Vassel (classes of 1732 and 1730), were Fellow Commoner gifts. Compliance of Fellow Commoners vis-à-vis presenting a piece of silver to the college was highest during the 1650s, when the practice of accepting such privileged students peaked. Reference to Fellow Commoners persisted through to the class of 1734, but it seems from 1654 onward the silver included items like a "beer bolwe," a "fruite dish" and a "sugar spoon." Perhaps the last time when the college silver was displayed at the induction of a new president was at Neil L. Rubenstein's installation as Harvard's twenty-sixth president in 1991. These valuables symbolized Harvard's continuity with its past. The signs of status had always been subtle—this effected a desired superiority. The patricians from Tory Row served a dish of India tea in their chambers and wore the same style of robes as the less affluent students, only silk. When the college divided over the lines of Loyalist and Patriots, the faculty ceased tea drinking altogether to curb the fighting.

THE GOODIES

Keeping students' quarters clean and tidy was a concern from the beginning of the college. At first, students had to do some finish carpentry on their own rooms, which were bought from them by the college when they graduated, and the housework was done by freshmen. Besides doffing their hats to everyone they passed crossing Harvard Yard and doing the bidding of upperclassmen, Harvard freshmen were obliged to help Mrs. Dunster with spring cleaning, using the same type of metal rug beater that has not been improved on today. A southerner who refused to comply with the assignment was told he could be expelled.

Then campus upkeep became a job done by maids who came from the town, and the minutes of a meeting of the corporation of March 1, 1659, noted that a maid was criticized about her work and that a butler was discharged.

In the era of President Eliot, never a stranger to social hierarchy and status, admissions catalogues had a budget for "Servants" next to rubrics for "Societies" and "Subscriptions to sports." There were clear social strata. Most students of the middle class lived in the quadrangle and had maid services seven days a week. Others fit into the Colonial Revival dorms of the Yard. Poorer students were consigned to off-campus boardinghouses. The wealthiest students lived in an elite set of unmarked buildings—the privately owned Westmorely Court, Randolph Hall, Apley Court, Claverly and Dudley on Mount Auburn Street—where they received all the services they wished to pay for. Randolph Hall (now part of Adams House, built in 1897) allegedly had chambers in the basement in 1950 known as "slave quarters." Here personal valets of princes and maharajas were said to store their inventory of Eastern luxuries such as Persian rugs and incense.

Above: Housekeepers of Harvard dorm room, circa 1871. *History Cambridge.*

Left: "Nelly." *Harvard University Libraries.*

Mothers were also barred from continuing to minister to their sons. Students could also not put their shoes outside the door to be polished—that was a job a gentleman could do for himself or at a shoeshine on the street.

In 1936, the maids joined a union, the UUERA, with other workers at the university. At that time, maids worked every day of the academic year except legal holidays. In 1940, they went to a six-day week, and the wage went up to forty-one cents per hour. Most privately endowed colleges in the East had in-house maid service before World War II. A new trend that followed the war was to abolish the service in favor of having each student make his own bed and getting the janitors to clean the rooms daily and vacuum weekly. Then Ivy League schools like Dartmouth, Brown, Yale and Princeton devised a policy where students replaced maids for some of the housekeeping in their dormitories. At Harvard, this was called the Student Porter system. An editor of the *Crimson* wrote in an article in 1951 that "the loss of the 9 a.m. cheeriness and relatively conscientious work of the maids is an unhappy prospect."[16]

Harvard, supposedly taking the concept from MIT, continued the same principle from 1979, recast as "Dorm Crew." A curious cleaning incident occurred that June. Several Dorm Crew members were cleaning out a room in Winthrop House when they discovered three letters written by Robert F. Kennedy (class of 1944) high on a top shelf at the back of a closet. They were turned in to the supervisor, Sheng-Bin Chiu (class of 1979). He graduated and returned home to Malaysia. Another student, Todd C. Hennis (class of 1982), said that he was "pretty sure" the letters were "simply filled with all the innocuous drivel one writes home to one's parents." He added, "It was great to touch a piece of history." The letters were never seen again.

The *Crimson* later reported that the letters, two on Winthrop House stationery and one with a military postmark, dated from the early 1940s. They mentioned Elsie's, the all-night diner; a clambake at Cape Cod; an intramural swim meet; and a date with Ethel for the Yale basketball game. One letter said to say hello to girlfriends back home. "School work was never discussed," said Henning P. Gutman (class of 1982), who was part of the crew that found the letters "way in the back where you had to jump up to reach."[17] Ted (Edward Moore) Kennedy, the ninth child of Joseph P. Kennedy Sr. and Rose, was the fourth brother to graduate from Harvard and the third to enter politics. He excelled in football and lived in Winthrop House, as had Jack and Bobby. Arriving in the fall of 1950 after a frolicsome summer in Europe, he drove around Cambridge in a Pontiac convertible with, wrote his biographer, a horn that bleated like a cow: "'I considered that fairly stylish and amusing,' he would remember. 'I was still a kid in many ways.'" He later would recall his behavior in college as very adolescent.[18]

When Ted had no time to study for his Spanish language class exam, Ted's football buddy found someone to sit for the exam in his place. No sooner had Ted walked out of the exam room than he was caught, and he and the exam proxy were expelled from Harvard. One year later, both were allowed to reapply, so Ted graduated in 1956, not in his original class. Six years later, he was elected a U.S. senator.

CHRIST CHURCH AND THE APTHORP HOUSE

Harvard's founding fathers saw themselves as non-separating Congregationalists from the state church ruled by the king. At Cambridge University, the Puritans were allowed to debate on religion. All the first six presidents of Harvard were ordained Puritan ministers. When there was a church project, like a new stone wall around the burial ground, the college and the town cooperated.

The early church buildings where Puritans worshiped in Cambridge are gone. Church of England (Anglican) members came to Cambridge nearly a century after the Puritans. They considered the fineness of their churches more important than did the Puritans, and the first Anglican Church building in Cambridge, Christ Church (1759–61), survives. Christ Church today is the oldest church building in the city; of the fourteen or more houses of worship within a third of a mile from the kiosk in Harvard Square, Christ Church can be said to have the closest historical association with Harvard.

By the mid-1700s, the religious homogeneity of Cambridge was ending. The Church of England Anglicans had lost their patience with having to go to Boston to church. They petitioned the Archbishop of Canterbury for a church and were sent young Reverend East Apthorp with the mandate to build one. Apthorp was from a wealthy Boston merchant family. His father traded in tea and slaves. The family had sent him to the University of Cambridge (England) after he finished at Boston Latin. Now young Apthorp was appointed missionary to Cambridge, Massachusetts.

He supervised the building of the church at the base of Garden Street during 1759–61 and returned his salary to its construction. It is a monument of early American architecture. The design, influenced by the Georgian style, was by Peter Harrison, architect of the King's Chapel in

Apthorp House (1760), photo from 1968. *Cambridge Historical Commission, Richard Cheek, photograph.*

Boston and the Touro Synagogue in Newport, Rhode Island. For himself, Apthorp also built a grand house in the Palladian style, which Reverend John Mayhew, a Boston Congregational minister, did not take kindly to, calling it a superb edifice, by which he meant ostentatious and unsuitable. The Congregationalists were upset looking at the mansion. They feared that because bishops were royal appointments, this Anglican priest might spy for George III. Thus, in 1775, before the foment of revolution, East Apthorp returned with his family to England. Not that he, his wife and four children suffered deprivation. Her brother was the mayor of London, and Apthorp got a series of high-powered appointments, including business head of St. Paul's Cathedral. After the surrender of the British, known as the Saratoga Convention, British general John Burgoyne was lodged in the Blue Anchor Tavern in Cambridge (marked by a plaque) and then at the Apthorp House, where, until he was released, he was required to buy all his furniture and pay rent.

Apthorp House is now one of the oldest houses in the city and a remarkable integration of town and gown, being enclosed within Adams House, 26 Plympton Street, and now the Master's Residence. This came about in the early 1900s, when Harvard was creating the house system of dormitories for

Christ Church, 1920. *Leon Abdalian, Boston Public Library.*

upperclassmen and Adams House, like Winthrop House, pulled together old
and new constructions. Most of the houses are grouped along the Charles
River, but Adams House was an exception, closer to the Yard. Reverend
Apthorp's house, the "Gold Coast" dormitories where wealthy students had
resided and new construction were merged into Adams House.

The minister who replaced Apthorp fled with his flock of Royalists to Halifax and then England. The interior of Christ Church was left unfinished.

Soon Washington's encampment in Cambridge brought a singular moment for Christ Church. Martha arrived in December 1775 in a coach and four black horses, with postilions and servants in scarlet livery. She quickly remarked on the disrepair of the church, then occupied by colonial troops, and requested the church be spruced up for a morning prayer service on the last day of the year. It was light but cold, and as was customary, servants of the congregation brought coals in braziers, which were played in the boxed pews. Washington agreed to attend, doubtless with some reluctance. This was a Royalist enclave and therefore an unpopular "Tory" faith was preached. Although he was a baptized member of the Church of England, Washington had been going to the Congregational meetinghouse. However, he went along with Martha's wishes and attended Christ Church with his staff and officers and their families. Historian Samuel F. Batchelder in his 1893 history of Christ Church suggested that General and Mrs. Washington occupied the sunny double-side enclosure box, state pew no. 17, which had before been occupied by Seir Francis Bernard, governor of Massachusetts from 1760 to 1769. At the New Year's Eve service, there was no Church of England rector, so the service was read by Colonel William Palfrey (memorialized by a tablet put up by his granddaughter), who prayed for the king (the sample portion of the long prayer follows):

Most heartily we beseech Thee to look down with mercy upon his Majesty George the Third. Open his eyes and enlighten his understanding, that he may pursue the true interest of the people over whom Thou in Thy Providence has placed him. Remove far from him all wicked, corrupt men, and evil counsellors, that his throne may be established in justice and righteousness.[19]

In a jovial letter of January 2 to his wife, who did not attend, Colonel Palfrey described his performance of divine service. "What think you of my turning parson?" he jested. He told her that he made up an original form of prayer for the king, which was much appreciated—the standard plea for his welfare but also asking the king to see the light about his people's true interests.[20] The church's organ had been smashed, and the lead of its pipes, being enemy property, had been melted for bullets during the Siege of Boston. Two military men accompanied the hymn singing on bass viola and clarinet.

Except for the service held for the Washingtons on December 31, 1775, the church was closed from 1774 to 1790, when it was fixed up and semi-reopened, with lay readers or temporary clergy. The Harvard faculty and students who were Episcopalians (the American church organized by former Anglicans after the Revolution) started holding services in the repaired building in 1790. Few of the original congregation of Loyalists were left. Harvard students, many from the South, could get excused from compulsory chapel by attending a Christ Church service. By the early nineteenth century, almost all the pews were rented and used again. In 1861, the centennial of the dedication of the church, the tower bell was replaced with thirteen bells, called the Harvard Chime, a gift by Harvard alumni including Richard Henry Dana, author of the sea adventure *Two Years Before the Mast*, who donated the novel's royalties. Episcopalian students started a group at Harvard called the St. Paul's Society, and the students gave Sunday sermons during Lent.

The practice of the reuse of Cambridge's houses of worship goes back to the late eighteenth century. The earliest reuse was that of Holden Chapel (1764) in Harvard Yard. Harvard didn't have a chapel for more than one hundred years after the college was founded. For the Puritans, each person was a temple; a plain meeting house suited them to confront their Maker. When Harvard Hall was built in 1766, religious services were conducted there instead of the more cramped Holden Chapel. During the American Revolution, Holden Chapel found a convenient use as a barracks. Who would have predicted that after the Revolution, skeletons would be stored in it for use by the first Harvard Medical School in 1782? Recently, the chapel has been used for student chamber music rehearsals and recitals.

Theodore Roosevelt, as a Harvard senior, was dismissed from teaching Sunday school at Christ Church. There are two stories as to why. An apocryphal story appears in Paul F. Boller's *Presidential Anecdotes*. It concerns a boy in TR's class who came one Sunday with a black eye. Hearing that the boy had got into a fistfight when an older boy pinched his little sister, TR rewarded him with a dollar. The vestry decided that the Harvard student was not suitable for religious education and he was dismissed.

A second version is documented by a letter to TR's mother, Martha Bulloch Roosevelt, written on January 11, 1880. "Darling Muffie," it began. He had received a grade of "very good" in an exam. He asked, "Please send my silk hat on at once: why has it not come before? Also send my rubbers on," and ended with the following news:

A good deal to my amusement and rather to my disgust I have been requested to resign my Sunday School Class unless I would Join the Episcopalian Church! This I refused to do, and so had to leave. I told the clergyman I thought him rather narrowminded especially as I had had my class for three years and a half, and as even he said it was the only boy's class in which attendance was at all regular. So now I have my afternoons to myself.[21]

Louise Ambler, the archivist of Christ Church, commented:

The new rector James Field Spaulding was a conservative and high church in his faith, a learned man for whom Latin and Greek were living languages. TR was a member of the Dutch Reformed Church from an old New York family. Spaulding said TR had to become Episcopalian if he taught Sunday school. There was no way that TR was converting. Spaulding fired him.[22]

Holden Chapel, built in 1744, etching circa 1875. In this tiny building, Professor Winthrop delivered public lectures. *Harvard University Archives.*

In line with TR's individualistic views, he also was critical of the biology instruction at Harvard. Judging the university as ignoring the science of outdoor naturalists, he turned away from a science major.

For more than 260 years, Christ Church has looked out over the Cambridge Common. Whereas once the parish looked inward, tending to the spiritual lives of especially the prominent citizens, it became from the 1950s a nexus and beacon for the community. The church in the 1950s was packed with worshipers, who also concentrated on issues of the City of Cambridge, of public recreation space, housing for the elderly, fluoridation, immigration and poverty. It soon became renowned for advancing civil rights, with parishioners marching to Washington and going on the Freedom Rally with Martin Luther King Jr. Christ Church members were early in protest of the Vietnam War, some marching to the statehouse with the American Civil Liberties Union. The church opened to participants in the rallies on the Common when others closed their doors. Reverend Day was interviewed by *TIME* magazine when it learned that he had denounced China's exclusion from the United Nations. Day was quoted as stating that "the church should speak out on all social, political, and economic matters. If you don't speak when the crisis is with you, you never get another chance."[23]

WHERE HAVE ALL THE FLOWERS GONE?

At the founding of the college, there was an abundance of cultivated men among the white English settlers who had come to New England to establish a godly society. About fifty settlers in the early villages of Massachusetts and Connecticut had degrees from Cambridge University in England. Elite schooling was a contributing factor to like-mindedness and a low level of dissent. In agreement about their high status, wealthy, educated Puritans predominated effortlessly. During the eighteenth century, the West Indian planters, cleaving together on Tory Row, were a vital economic force. But while one day at late eighteenth-century Cambridge Tory Row was a solidly rich enclave, the next day it was vacated, with few returning after the Revolution for fear of reprisals.

A similar like-mindedness of polite or at least law-abiding behavior characterized the nascent British colony in Canada at the end of the eighteenth century. Most of the Loyalists who fled America ended up in the more obedient and better-mannered British maritime colonies, especially

General Howe's evacuation from Boston, March 17, 1776. *Amon Carter Museum of American Art, Fort Worth, Texas.*

the towns of Halifax, Nova Scotia and St. John, New Brunswick. The broad concern of the several thousand refugees whom the British navy deposited was to form a peaceable society along the lines of the old social hierarchy. Some of the oldest Harvard graduates continued to make new lives in England, with some returning with official positions bestowed by the Crown. Meanwhile, it is no exaggeration to state that St. John became run by an oligarchy that initially was a "Little Harvard."

In a Founders' Day Address at the University of New Brunswick, Clifford K. Shipton, director of the American Antiquarian Society, stated:

> *It might be said that colleges sprang up in the footprints of the Puritans. One of the first acts of the settlers of Massachusetts Bay was to found Harvard College, and wherever the sons of Harvard and Yale went, north, west, or south, colleges sprang up in their footsteps. These men knew well that even the imperfect democracy of the communities from which they came could not survive without an educated public. If William Paine had not taken the first step to found the institution which has grown into this University, some other members of the group of Harvard graduates in the Province would have done so.*[24]

71

Whereas the church and state had been one in early New England, the Anglican Church was removed from politics in Canada. Not church dogma but class held the newcomers together, and initially the Harvard graduates filled the bill as a powerful gentlemen's club. Some got government positions. Others set up law practices (problems of land distribution required lawyers to sort things out). Members of Little Harvard competed with one another for plum positions and socialized together. They worshiped at the same Anglican church and continued friendships established on Brattle Street and Beacon Hill. Many not only shared Harvard as an alma mater but also were of the same college generation. Not that all the Ivies were minted in Cambridge, Massachusetts— Jonathan Odell, who became a provincial secretary, graduated from Princeton.

An Ivy imprimatur had added significance because some of the Loyalists arrived with only the shirts on their backs. Those who had fought the war on the British side as common soldiers were glad to farm, but the Harvard men did not have survival skills. They strove to fulfill their Harvard promise often on slight means and a little help from their relatives who had chosen the winning side. Among themselves they were competitive for the provincial positions.

The roster of "Little Harvard" included Ward Chipman, a protégé of Attorney General Jonathan Sewell at the time of the Revolution. On September 1, 1774, British soldiers headed up the Mystic River into Boston and removed barrels of gunpowder that the rebels had stored from a powder house. That afternoon, Chipman was at Sewell's house doing legal business when an angry crowd gathered outside. Someone fired a shot from the second story that set off an attack from the mob. Windows were broken and rocks thrown. One week later, Sewell, his family and Chipman fled and were among the seven thousand Loyalists who made the reverse migration to London in 1775 and 1776.

Jonathan Sewell missed his chance to go to Harvard due to war, but his father had attended. The elder Jonathan Sewell replaced the *a* in his surname with a second *e* for no known reason once he got to England. Jonathan the son was eight when the family's Brattle Street mansion was sacked. He did not, for obvious reasons, follow his father's footsteps to Harvard. After one year at Cambridge University, he began his legal career in St. John in the Province of New Brunswick.

Jonathan Bliss (Harvard class of 1762) studied law with old family friend Ward Chipman, who had become solicitor general of Canada, and fulfilled his family's destiny in public life, albeit in New Brunswick rather than Massachusetts. Bliss and Chipman were elected to the first New

Brunswick legislature. The election was grossly unfair. The sheriff closed the polls at a designated poll site in the commercial downtown of St. John (before Fredericton was the provincial capital) and disallowed votes from the opposing candidates. As a result, many poor and liberal people quit the province, leaving it top heavy with high-status people.

Another prestigious member of the unofficial club, along with his brother and father, was Dr. William Paine (Harvard class of 1768). His schoolmaster of Latin as a boy was John Adams. Although Dr. Paine was licensed by the Crown to vaccinate against smallpox, the Town of Salem denied him the practice. When he heard that Governor Hutchinson was evacuating Boston, he sailed back to England, received a new medical degree in Aberdeen, accompanied an aristocrat to Lisbon as his personal physician, was admitted to the Royal College of Physicians and became a popular doctor to the upper class in England. Guy Carleton appointed Dr. Paine Physician to the army and assigned him to Halifax, where he could retire at half pay on a land grant in New Brunswick. He was the first petitioner to sign the document for the founding of the University of New Brunswick in 1785 and in 1787 received Carleton's permission to move back to Salem, Massachusetts. It is notable that such a powerful figure suffered, as did many of the displaced Loyalists, from impoverishment—his patients couldn't pay for his services.

Not every Harvard graduate who fled to Halifax and eastern Canada achieved lasting, restored prestige after the Revolution. Benjamin Marston (class of 1749) had a business in Marblehead with two brothers-in-law before the Revolution. In Nova Scotia and New Brunswick, he became a surveyor, an influential position during the disposition of land grants in Canada, but this did not go well. The governor ordered Black residents who had left America for their freedom to be placed in Northwest Harbor (New Brunswick), but the disbanded soldiers rioted and destroyed the residents' homes, fearing that their salaries would be undercut. Marston became a scapegoat for the riot, after which he served as a surveyor in the region of Miramachi, then the biggest town of New Brunswick. While a merchant and supercargo in the West India trade, he was captured three times by pirates and traded to freedom. He took the post of chief surveyor for a private company in West Africa but grew sick and died on the voyage.

Harvard connections of Loyalists who adventured and struggled in their exile are manifold. John Wentworth (class of 1768), surveyor of the King's Woods in the Maritimes, made Marston his deputy in New Brunswick and went to live in St. John, where he shared a house with Ward Chipman. When

Edward Winslow (class of 1741) asked for compensation from the British government for being a Loyalist in March 1787, Marston went to Boston to obtain documentation in support of the Winslow family's claim. These self-exiled men shared tips on gardening and gout, banqueted together, got each other jobs as magistrates and intermarried.

The influx of Harvard graduates at the very beginning of New Brunswick's history left its mark on succeeding generations as well. Harvard was a mecca for Canadian Maritime Province students in the nineteenth century. Many of the leading Loyalists who founded Nova Scotia and New Brunswick retained an affection for their homeland, so the drift of bright students from well-to-do families to established universities in the United States was natural.

Premier historian of Maritime Canada Ronald Rees noted:

> *For some, such as the botanist W.F. Ganong and Bliss Carman, later a renowned poet, Harvard was a finishing school where they went for more prestigious degrees than those offered by the University of New Brunswick, then King's College. Both Carman and Ganong had King's College and Harvard BAs, and Carman contributed regularly to "Harvard Monthly." In 1889, Ganong reported that sixteen of the twenty Canadian students at Harvard were from Maritime universities and all the Canadian students in the arts and humanities were Maritimers. So were all the Canadian teachers on the Harvard staff.* [25]

Edward Winslow's family came over on the *Mayflower* and had a tradition of public office and social influence on the South Shore of Massachusetts. Winslow (Harvard class of 1765) put himself forward to hold high public office in New Brunswick. He joined the British army, became a lieutenant colonel, was popular and witty and was the author of important letters; however, he was always short of funds.

John Wentworth (Harvard class of 1755) was the governor of New Hampshire before the Revolution. His big project was for New Hampshire to have a college equal to Massachusetts. He rode with his friends on horseback to Dartmouth every class day and presented the college with a silver bowl that is still in Dartmouth's possession. Wentworth was an able frontiersman who spent seasons in the wilderness surveying for the Crown in Canada, but he also with his wife, Fanny, upheld the aristocratic customs, furnishing their home in Halifax and giving balls and galas that even impressed Prince William, the third son of George III. Wentworth seems to have looked the other way when the prince had a fling with his wife during a visit on a naval tour.

The self-exiled Loyalists valued the undisturbed state of life, retired from warfare and political dissension, yet daily life was hard and there was class dissension. St. John was rough and ready due to the thousands of British veteran soldiers trying to establish viable opportunities for their families. The more aristocratic refugees distanced themselves from St. John and bought houses, often second houses, in St. Andrews and Fredericton. The wish to have a great university began and continued in Fredericton. Meanwhile, Cambridge connected the Maritime Provinces with the rest of New England by both legal trade and smuggling. For the most part, the society was composed of people who had learned to value a retirement from dissension.

BRIDGES

The Great Bridge across the Charles was built by the Puritans in 1662 at the foot of Boylston Street, on the site of the present Anderson Bridge. Building bridges across the Charles involved Cambridge-Boston politics from the start. The Cambridge shore was isolated in the eighteenth century, being bordered by salt marshes with low ground and access only by boat or going by way of Charlestown and Roxbury. In 1738, Harvard opposed a new bridge between Cambridge and Boston:

> [A]ny nearer and more ready Passage, over said River and especially by a Bridge, will cause such an increase of Company etc. at the College, that thereby the Scholars will be in danger of being too much interrupted in their Studies and hurt in their Morals.[26]

Chief Justice Francis Dana was a major figure in bringing a fine bridge across the Charles to Cambridge. He had an unabashed personal interest, as he had a great deal of property in east Cambridge. Opponents maintained that rich gentlemen were out to destroy trade from Charlestown and the North End and make their estates more accessible. The West Boston Bridge, which opened in 1793, reduced the distance from the statehouse and North Church to Cambridge from eight to three miles and led to the development of Cambridgeport. It was replaced by the Longfellow Bridge, which opened in 1906 as the Cambridge Bridge and was renamed the Longfellow Bridge in 1927 in honor of the poet, who was inspired to write his poem "The Bridge" for it:

How often, O, how often,
In the days that had gone by,
I had stood on that bridge at midnight
And gazed on that wave and sky!

The Longfellow Bridge connects Boston and Kendall Square, Cambridge. It is known as the Salt-and-Pepper bridge because the central pillars resemble salt and pepper shakers, each one having a handsome Viking prow near the waterline.

The first substantial bridge to have crossed the Charles River between the marshes of Cambridge and Boston was the West Boston Bridge. Charles Sullivan, executive director of the Cambridge Historical Commission, wrote in *A City's Life and Times*, "The opening of the West Boston Bridge in 1793 ended Cambridge's isolation from Boston and triggered the town's first real estate boom." The landscape of pasture and farmland and the development of Cambridge to the east of the original village and the college began.[27]

The most historic bridges that connect Boston and Cambridge are the Longfellow Bridge (1906, replacing the West Boston Bridge), the Anderson Bridge (1915), the John W. Weeks Bridge (1927) and the Eliot Bridge (1950).

Harvard Stadium, a U-shaped stadium in Allston, opened in 1903 and was an early achievement of a large-scale construction in reinforced concrete. Like a big new piece of furniture being brought into a house, the stadium necessitated more adjustments. The old timber bridge that went from Allston to Boston had been rebuilt several times since the initial Great Bridge of 1660 but was still inadequate. The university and the city were also cognizant of the riverfront's potential for development. However, the City of Boston refused to pay for anything better than a plain wooden drawbridge, maintaining that mainly Cambridge's interests would be served. Moreover, the War Department required either a draw or a twenty-seven-foot vertical clearance, which would make the approaching roads lengthy and costly.

Harvard president Eliot wrote to President Theodore Roosevelt (class of 1880) that this was a favorable juncture to persuade the federal government to create a new bridge. Eliot attended a bridge construction hearing with architects, professors and several Cambridge aldermen. Things moved ahead, and a design competition was held in 1908. However, a low-level bridge would obstruct users of the upper Charles (e.g., the Watertown Arsenal, a depot for coal barges and the wharf of an abattoir). Delegations

"Going to the Harvard-Yale Game," circa 1907. Harvard students in great numbers crossing the Anderson Bridge on their way to the Harvard Stadium. *Cambridge Historical Commission Postcard Collection.*

of lobbyists on both sides, bridge or no bridge, were contesting the plan in Congress when it was saved by the Cambridge Police and the Harvard-Yale football game.

Newly elected president W.H. Taft was a graduate of Harvard Law School and the father of Senator Taft, who in 1918 also graduated from the law school. President Taft was a great traveler, and he wanted to squeeze in attending the 1910 Harvard-Yale football game on the Fourth of July before other commitments and whistle-stops across the land. It is said that Taft weighed three times as much as President James Madison, but it is acknowledged he had great vigor, exerted for example in his anti-trust activities. The stadium had a capacity of twenty-three thousand, and on game days the bridge was exceedingly crowded. A *Harvard Lampoon* cartoon represented the bridge timbers sagging under the weight of football crowds, while the Skeleton Death was "beckoning expectantly." The president would be obliged to cross the Charles to the stadium on the ailing bridge—perhaps Taft's weight caused the police to consider the weight-bearing capacity of the bridge. In any case, the Cambridge Police refused to take responsibility for his safety, and so the matter was resolved—a new arch bridge soon spanned the river where the 1662 Great Bridge had preceded it. It is of a closed-spandrel type without columns at the edges where the bridge meets the land, giving it an even, graceful aesthetic. It took its name of Anderson Bridge from

Anderson Memorial Bridge. *Scott Eisen.*

The Weeks Bridge, 1926, McKim, Mead & White, architects, at its dedication on May 17, 1927. *Cambridge Historical Commission, International Newsreel photo.*

Nicholas Longworth Anderson, a Civil War veteran and diplomat (Harvard class of 1858) whose son Larz covered the whole cost. The architects were Iran Hollis and L.J. Johnson with McKim, Mead & White.

Downstream, the university constructed the Weeks Bridge in 1926, a pedestrian bridge that also carried steam heat to the new Harvard Business School across the river. John Wingate Weeks, secretary of war under Presidents Harding and Coolidge, was the namesake, and his business associates had raised the funds for its construction.

The Eliot Bridge—a brick-faced, concrete arch bridge between Cambridge and Allston that was built in 1950 as a memorial to C.W. Eliot, president of Harvard from 1869 to 1909, and his son Charles Eliot, a landscape architect for Boston's Metropolitan Park Commission—connects Soldier's Field in Alston with Memorial Drive and Fresh Pond Parkway.

Part III

THE NINETEENTH CENTURY

*H*omo faber was an ideal of the Victorian age. Longfellow labored over his rhymes about rural people as the locality urbanized, while the town and Harvard became fertile places for industry and invention, such as machinist Elias Howe's lockstitch sewing machine, developed in his father's Cambridge factory in 1846, and the "Reversible Collar," patented by George K. Snow in 1866. This chapter samples industries before turning to events at Harvard.

THE CANDY FACTORY

New England Confectionery Company (Necco), founded in 1847, is the oldest candy producer in America. Originally in South Boston, the forerunner was Chase & Company. Oliver R. Chase invented and patented the first candy machine, the lozenge cutter, which allowed thin candies to be snipped off a pipe before hardening. A family of three companies joined to form Necco in 1902.

The familiar Necco wafers themselves were made from 1844 in Cambridge first near the MIT campus on Massachusetts Avenue, then in Lechmere Square. The factory moved to an 810,000-square-foot location in Revere, Massachusetts, in 2003, but for a century there was a familiar candy smell in the area around the factory. The company offered profit sharing benefits from 1906 and in 1920 insured all candy-makers.

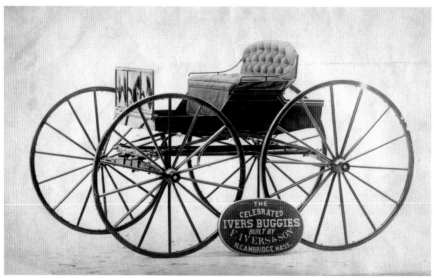

Opposite, top: "Winter Scene," Massachusetts Avenue looking east, 1890. *History Cambridge.*

Opposite, bottom: Francis Ivers & Sons was at the corner of Allen Street and Massachusetts Avenue. Established in 1856, it specialized in production of the Ivers buggy and other light road carriages. *History Cambridge.*

Above: Delivery truck for Lever Brothers Company advertising Lux toilet soap (164 Broadway), undated. *Cambridge Historical Commission Ephemera Collection.*

The company was responsible for many classic candies on the American scene, including Clark Bars, Canada Mints, pecan fudge, marshmallow chocolates, caramels and Mary Janes. Pictures of the old factory show an "enrobing room" where the chocolate coverings were done.

Necco wafers were packaged in waxed paper rolls from 1912. Each roll had a variety of pastel discs in different flavors. With slight variations (cinnamon has come and gone), they are identifiable as lemon (yellow), lime (green), wintergreen (pink), orange (orange), licorice (dark gray), clove (light purple), cinnamon (white) and chocolate (brown). They are the company's signature. Because they don't melt and were neatly packaged, Admiral Bird took two and a half tons of Necco wafers to the South Pole, a pound a week for each of the men during their two-year expedition of 1928–30. During World War II, the U.S. government put Necco wafers in soldiers' rations.

The tiny colored hearts date from the mid-nineteenth century. During the Civil War, a love interest might receive a candy heart with a piece of paper inside, printed with "Please send a lock of your hair by return mail." The printed messages on the Necco colored hearts had to be contained in a half inch of space—popular messages included "Yours 4 ever," "Sweet talk" and "You shine," as well as the bolder "U R Hot." It was once national news when messages were added to the tiny colored hearts, such as "Te Amo" and "Je t'aime" and, just recently, "Tweet me."

When Necco failed, the Spangler Company purchased it out of bankruptcy and revived the candies, announcing that it was going to have a richer brown chocolate wafer.

A giant "Necco" was unveiled on a water tower to mark the candy's 150th anniversary in 1997. The following year, an intriguing small metal sculpture by artist Ross Miller, which features the wafers and conversation hearts, was installed as part of MIT's University Park, near Central Square. It features wafers and conversation hearts and is mounted on a boulder in the park's northeast corner. The old factory today is the headquarters to Novartis Pharma, a biomedical research firm.

NEW ENGLAND GLASS

In the face of a shortage of imported goods during the War of 1812, a glassworks was established in East Cambridge in 1814 to produce fine tableware. When the property was put up for sale in 1817, the New England Glass Company took it over and operated in East Cambridge until 1888. It became the most important glass plant in the country, and examples of its glass are now in museum collections, including the Metropolitan Museum of Art. The engraving of an important presentation vase of the company's manufacture (1843) at the Metropolitan depicts the New England Glass Company with the chimneys of its three furnaces—two for glass and one for lead.

The supervisor of the glassworks and many of the workers came from a glassworks in Edinburgh during the 1820s. By 1835, a Harvard professor observed, "The men employed to make the glass are I believe all Scotch men." The company concentrated on a refined type of glass called flint

This presentation vase of blown, cut and engraved glass, 1843, bears a depiction of the New England Glass Company, with the chimneys of its three furnaces, two for glass and one for lead. *Metropolitan Museum of Art.*

glass made with lead oxide. Lead's high refractive index imparted a brilliance to the pieces, which were mostly clear and later also colored. Flint glass was also more suitable to cutting compared with potash glass.

An article about New England Glass appeared in *Gleason's Pictorial and Drawing Room Companion*, a midcentury weekly newspaper: "There is hardly a home from Maine to Louisiana which has not more or less of this excellent ware in domestic use. Every description of glassware, from a simple pressed glass wine glass to the most elaborately cut and richly plated, gilded, silvered and engraved glass is produced in a style of beauty and excellence unrivalled in the world."[1]

The glassworks became the largest in the world, with five furnaces and ten pots capable of holding two thousand pounds each of molten glass. The factory chimney of 230 feet in height was 10 feet higher than Bunker Hill Monument and visible from everywhere in Cambridge. The chimney was connected by underground tubes to the furnaces so that the smoke and gasses were carried off into the air at a great height. The glasswork was very successful, and apparently some profit went to the workers.

Glassmaking ran in families, with third generations of men not uncommon. The life of a glassmaker was hard. The excessive heat to melt the glass, the gases breathed into the lungs and the tremendous pressure necessary to blow the glass made the mortality percentage high.

In early years, when a piece of molded glass was being made, the hinged iron mold was slipped around the red-hot bubble and the blower took it again. As he blew, the hot glass filled the surfaces of the mold. Then the mold was removed and the blower's tube broken away from the bottom of the piece. A resulting "punt mark" was characteristic of the early molded glass, like on blown glass. On the later pieces of poured or molded glass, the bottoms were smoothly finished, as the tube was not used. The piece was then set on the shelf of a cooler oven to harden for up to five days. The quality and resistance to chipping of fine glass was due to slow, careful cooling and hardening. The plant started by making blown flint glass—that is, glass in which silica is the main ingredient. Silica was made in England from calcined and pulverized flints. Oxide of lead was also added to make the glass refractive and brilliant.

A specialty was colored glass, a type of antique Bohemian, but the East Cambridge plant excelled in engraved, cut and silvered products. Some of the molded glass shared patterns made at Sandwich, Massachusetts, as was very natural since ideas and workers were mingled.

In 1827, the pressing mold for glass was invented by a workman named Robinson at the New England factory. This humanitarian and labor-saving device, which completely altered a great industry, was, like the sewing machine, invented in Cambridge.

At the Columbia Centennial in 1825, New England Glass advertised window glass, entry lamps, the fashionable new astral lamps and sconces with cut glass founts. The glass work flourished in East Cambridge until

Covered sugar bowl, blown, finished by tooling, circa 1830. *Richard Goodbody, Toledo Art Museum.*

the 1870s, when the business slumped, but a "gaffer" from England who had had much experience in colored glass came to the factory and business picked up again. There was a call for molded glass among the people who could not afford cut glass.

Objects like the sugar bowl shown here date from the 1830s, when pressed glass had progressed from flat to shapes. It was made when the influence of the craft of flint glass from Scotland was high. Decorations were ample, for aesthetics and because lacelike patterns and stippling concealed imperfections.

By midcentury, there were 450 workmen employed in the plant in thirteen buildings. In 1888, when the New England Glass Company was sold due to a financial downturn, it moved to Ohio. The new owner, a Mr. Libbey, had long been employed at the Cambridge plant. He stressed the new cut glass that was just coming into vogue, and his product later became internationally famous for its beauty and fine quality as "Libbey cut glass."

Professor Horsford

Academics can live in their own world, and their institutions seem to have more "characters" than other segments of society. Regarding eccentrics on college campuses, a token one can stand for the many. Eben N. Horsford was a professor of chemistry at Harvard for sixteen years. Horsford was trained as a civil engineer at Rensselaer and became an expert in the chemistry of foods after advanced study in Germany. Horsford received an appointment at Harvard as Rumford Professor on the Application of Science to the Useful Arts in 1847. Like Horsford, the chair's namesake had inventions in a wide range of domains. He was Benjamin Thompson, the Woburn farm boy whose attendance at Professor Winthrop's lectures was mentioned earlier and who rose to be Count Rumford of the Holy Roman Empire. Thompson/Rumford invented the Rumford fireplace, Rumford soup and the crouton while in exile, as he was a Royalist.

Horsford likewise developed many chemical processes on topics including condensed milk and emergency rations; the advances he made in leavening bread from 1854 made him famous and rich. Before Horsford's innovation, leaveners were added to dough, which rose on the counter before baking. Thanks to his improvements, instead of fizzing out rapidly, the leavening principle in the baking powder lasted during baking. Now the dough was more elastic and springier (twice as fizzy) and less bitter. His secret was a chemical adjustment of replacing cream of tartar with calcium acid phosphate. He derived this first from bone and then synthetically. The professor's formulation emitted the teeny bubbles that leavening causes, and in reaction to heat, the formulation rose a second time. He obtained patents to produce calcium acid phosphate as well as other chemicals and kept improving his formula, adding cornstarch as a buffer to the soda and the acid. The double-acting baking powder was also dry and shelf stable, so that its leavening property recovered when heated. This was only one of the professor's avenues of food research to help the Union army during the Civil War and, of course, acquire government contracts.

The professor had also named his company in Providence after Count Rumford, calling it the Rumford Chemical Works. By the 1870s, Horsford had sold his shares in the enterprise to his business partner and left teaching. It was at this juncture that he became infatuated with the Vikings and the mythical city of Norumbega—he was a very rich man with time on his hands.

Obsessive in the pursuit of results in the laboratory, Horsford developed a mania. This happened when he went to a concert of the famous Norwegian violinist Ole Bull. Bull believed that Leif Erikson had visited North America and that the magical North American kingdom of Norumbega was located along the New England coast. The professor was enthralled. He set out to prove that Erikson had sailed up the Charles River and explored the Charles River Basin, which covers many miles of eastern Massachusetts. He excavated and found what he contended were Viking relics and claimed that the Norse sagas described specific places in the Charles River Basin. Horsford also invented Norse etymologies for Native American names. He wrote books on his theories about Norumbega and erected monuments to the Vikings in Cambridge and Weston and Boston. A plaque can be seen by a walker along Fresh Pond Parkway with Gerry's Landing Road to the left. It reads,

Trade card for Horsford's Acid Phosphate, Rumford Chemical Works, 58, 59 and 60 South Water Street, Providence, Rhode Island. The product was for treating mental and physical exhaustion and dyspepsia. Verso reads, "Prepared according to directions of Prof. E.N. Horsford of Cambridge, MA." *Historic New England.*

"On this spot in the year 1000 Leif Erickson built his house in Vineland."

Horsford believed that the magical kingdom had been near Weston. His monument to the Norse there is Norumbega Tower (1889), located at the confluence of Stony Brook and the Charles River; thirty-eight feet tall, it bears a plaque declaring his claim that this was the location of Fort Norumbega. The tower is sixty steps to the top and has been ascended on special occasions when the Parks Commission opens it. Another plaque sits in the corner of the lawns of Cambridge's Mount Auburn Hospital. The professor also served on the committee to promote the erection of the Leif Erikson statue.

Bull stayed with fellow Viking enthusiast Henry Wadsworth Longfellow at his Cambridge house when he visited Boston, and the plan of where to place the statue was resolved over dinner attended by Bull, Longfellow and Longfellow's brother-in-law, Thomas Gold Appleton. Longfellow had published "Skeleton in Armor" with a Viking as the central character, set in Massachusetts. The poem was inspired by a skeleton wearing a metal breastplate that had been unearthed in a sand bank behind a meetinghouse in Fall River in 1832. In Longfellow's ode, this was the skeleton of a Viking who had escaped with his beloved across the Atlantic and lived in exile.

Boston's most prominent citizens promoted the Erikson statue plan until they saw the model of what the sculptor, John Quincy Adams Ward, intended: a bearskin-draped Viking warrior. Moreover, the Massachusetts Horticultural Society maintained that there was insufficient evidence that Norsemen discovered America. A few years later, Horsford revived the project, thus an eight-foot statue of Leif Erikson, commissioned from Anne Whitney by Horsford, stands high on a pedestal at the far western end of the Commonwealth Avenue promenade in Boston. It has at its base a stonework boat. On the sculpture's dedication in the fall of 1887, there was a parade in Boston, and Governor Oliver Ames spoke at Faneuil Hall. At that time, the figure on its pedestal could be seen from the river. A copy was placed in Juneau Park in Milwaukee, where the Vikings were supposed to have reached.

Horsford's romance with the Vikings apparently was perverted by other nineteenth-century luminaries, including the professor's friend Thomas Gold Appleton (in his "A Sheaf of Papers," 1875), to promote white supremacy theories.

Horsford and his first wife met when she was his pupil in a female academy. They had four children. When she died, he married his sister-in-law and had another daughter. As the father of five daughters, he took an interest in higher education for women, and he was a major contributor to Wellesley College, founded in 1879.

The grave of the baking powder magnate is at the edge of Cambridge Common in the Old Burying Ground. Today, Horford's company has changed hands, but Rumford baking powder is still made in Terre Haute at the Clabber Girl Corporation (part of B&G Foods).

LEVER SOAP

In Greek mythology, the Olympian god of invention is Hephaistos. A patron of blacksmiths, metalworkers and stonemasons, and despite a busy romantic life, Hephaistos was a technical wonder in Elysium. Instead of lounging on a cloud like most of his fellows, Hephaistos was unique in making devices for heavenly use—driverless carts, tables on wheels, automatic bellows and even an automatic opener for the heavenly gates. Hephaistos could be the patron of Kendall Square too, given that the latest iteration of the industrial part of Cambridge has more than 150 biotech, IT, clean energy and other tech companies. Regarding the development of the city of Cambridge's eastern flank, Hephaistos seems to have played with mortals by tossing down and removing buildings and bringing extraordinary changes.

This area, which is now partly East Cambridge and partly Cambridgeport, was brackish terrain through Victorian times, when the marshes were filled in and Cambridge extended east. The former riverside areas took the name of "Old Port" or "the Port," and thanks to two bridges—the North Bridge and one that preceded the Longfellow at that location—the area became industrial. From then on, the ever-fickle Hephaistos planted every manner of enterprise there, from the manufacture of table tennis paddles to that of Polaroid cameras, pianos and fountain pens, the common factor being industries requiring skilled factory workers, supplied by the immigrants who moved in or commuted from Boston.

A pivotal moment was created by the War of 1812, which brought a blockade to the Eastern Seaboard. Subsequently, the historic purlieus of Kendall Square were transformed in response to the biotech revolution. In *MIT Technology Review* magazine, Alice Dragoon elaborated on the high-tech trajectory (in summary):

> *Biogen moved into a warehouse on Binney Street in 1983. The Whitehead Institute, which would help head the Human Genome Project, arrived in 1984, followed by Genzyme in 1990 [acquired by Sanofi in 2011]; the corner of Vassar and Maine is a nexus of the life sciences, with the Broad Institute, the Mc Govern Institute for Brain Research, the Picower Institute for Learning and Memory, the Koch Institute for Integrative Cancer Research, the Whitehead, and Novartis all within shouting distance of one another; Microsoft and Google have a presence; and there are 600 startups at the Cambridge Innovation Center at One Broadway. The immediate Kendall Square vicinity has 50 attractive restaurants often with outdoor dining in plazas.*[2]

That the space was industrial and minimally residential permitted all this to happen rapidly. Each of the prior factories has a human history. The biggest was the Lever Brothers soap factory, encompassing thirty buildings at Portland Street and Broadway beginning in 1898. Lever Brothers was

"Writes a strong rich blue." Advertisement for Carter's Ink Company ink from the *Literary Digest*, May 10, 1919. Gift of John Hinkel, Carter's Ink Company Collection. *Cambridge Historical Commission.*

an English company in origin; some of its product lines were Life Buoy and Lux. It had created Sunshine Village near Liverpool in the 1880s to accommodate soap workers, complete with the Lady Lever Art Gallery for their education. The sizable village was like the planned mill towns of New England, while at the same time Lever Brothers relied on mostly plantations in the African Congo, where palm oil was extracted using forced labor. The company was established in Cambridge by the hubristic and despotic William Lever, who had been given the title First Viscount Leverhulme by Queen Victoria.

Leverhulme figured in the European and American public imagination as a tycoon of strictest probity. He dictated a letter quickly to three stenographers so together they would catch every word, and when he traveled from his estate to London, he had people he wished to do business with travel in vehicles following his; when he had terminated his instructions to one person, that person got out and went into one of the other cars, to be replaced by someone else. Meanwhile, on the plantations, workers not only starved and lived in horrid conditions but also were denigrated by the viscount as "lazy donkeys." What made him the worst type of robber baron is that when he traveled to the Belgian Congo, he was very merry about those he abused, saying that someday they might rise to the white man's level but until then were children.

The plant employed 1,300 workers through the 1920s. Lever Brothers had pioneered soaps of vegetable fat (as opposed to tallow, or animal-based fat), but the plant was closed because it could not be repurposed when synthetic soaps gained popular approval. It had dominated the scene, and its shift of its headquarters to New York in 1969 dealt Cambridge an economic blow. It was then that the city and MIT collaborated on the fruitful idea of converting the vacated site into a research park.

Adjacent to MIT is Tech Square, an office building complex with this sleek no-nonsense name, corresponding to the intellectual mindset of scientists, mathematicians and engineers associated with the institute.

Homages to the past thread through the MIT campus. The handsome Polaroid building is still at 780 Memorial Drive. Number 250 Massachusetts Avenue, once a whole block of East Cambridge that smelled of candy, is now offices, while the seven-acre American Rubber Company at 680 Massachusetts Avenue, founded in 1872, had 1,500 employees making rubber heels, boots and clothes. It has been converted to high-end apartments.

THE HASTY PUDDING

The oldest social club in America is the Hasty Pudding. Five U.S. presidents (John and John Quincy Adams, Theodore Roosevelt and Franklin Delano Roosevelt and John F. Kennedy) have been members, as well as others who achieved fame. For some members, like Jack Lemmon (class of 1947), its theatricals pointed the way to a dramatic career. For others, like architect H.H. Richardson, the connections made through the club led to potential clients.

It was early fall when twenty-one juniors of the class of 1797 gathered in Nymphas Hatch's dorm room and formed a secret society. All had been born during the American Revolution. In the spirit of levity, they pledged that the members were, in alphabetical order, bound to provide a pot of hasty pudding for each meeting. It required two students to carry a cast-iron pot of the dessert from the refectory kitchen across the Yard.

Joel Barlow's *The Hasty-Pudding* appears in anthologies of old American poetry. Barlow was a chaplain in the Revolutionary War, founder of the Connecticut weekly *American Mercury* and, while consul at Algiers, helped draft the Treaty of Tripoli and free merchant sailors from Barbary pirates.

Hasty-Pudding-Club.

TAFT'S HOTEL,

WEST ROXBURY.

GAME SUPPER

FOR

THIRTY GENTLEMEN.

January 13th, 1854.

BILL OF FARE.

Oysters on Shell.

ROAST.

Black-head Ducks, from Virginia,	Sprig-tail Ducks, from Georgia,
Wild Turkey, from Illinois,	Brant, from Delaware,
Red-head Ducks,	Green-wing Teel,
Wild Goose,	Blue-wing Teel,
Black Ducks,	Widgeon Teel,
Gray Ducks,	Quails, Larded,
Blue-bill Widgeon,	Partridges, Larded,
Canvas-back Ducks,	Grouse, from Illinois,
Mallard Ducks, from N. Carolina,	Spruce Partridges, from Canada.

English Hare, per last Steamer,
Venison, with Grape and Currant Jelly.

PUDDINGS.

Custard,   Bread.

PASTRY.

Meat Pies,	Squash Pies,
Apple Pies,	Lemon Pies.

ICE CREAMS.

Sherbet,	Strawberry,
Lemon,	Vanilla.

Calf's Foot Jelly, Blanc Mange.

DESSERT.

Grapes,   Pears,   Apples,   Raisins,   Dry Fruit.

COFFEE.

H. P. C. from R. C. Winthrop, Jr. 1691.

Hasty Pudding Club at Taft's Hotel. "Game Supper for Thirty Gentlemen," January 1854. *Harvard University Libraries.*

Although not written by a member of the Harvard club—Barlow went to Yale—it has a perfectly collegiate tone:

Let the green Succatash with thee contend.
Let beans and corn their sweetest juices blend,
Let butter drench them in its yellow tide.
And a long slice of bacon grace their side;
Not all the plate, how fam'd soe'er it be,
Can please my palate like a bowl of thee.

Hasty Pudding meetings were enlivened with mock trials, some spoofing happenings in Cambridge and among the faculty. By 1860, the trials had evolved into shows. The poet James Russell Lowell was the first to cross-dress head to toe in 1837 when he played Abby Row in a breach of promise suit. The year 1867 marked the first student-written play, *Dido and Aeneas*, written by Owen Wister, who would write the first American western, *The Virginian*, in 1902. The play *Dido and Aeneas* was a great success and was taken on tour across the country.

In 1917, a meeting to plan the annual Hasty Pudding production saw a unanimous vote to enlist instead. Shows were canceled for two years; of members who went to war, a dozen were wounded and fifteen died.

Beginning in 1950, the club honored movie stars and invited them to a gala. The first Woman of the Year was stage actress Gertrude Lawrence; the first time the elected entertainer was male was Bob Hope in 1967. Jack Lemmon had practice acting in women's clothes in a Hasty Pudding show before *Some Like It Hot*. He was Man of the Year in 1973, after Dustin Hoffman and before Peter Falk.

Connected with the club's history is that of Harvard's venerable a capella group, the Krokodiloes. A custom evolved after the Civil War for Hasty Pudding members to sing popular college songs after meetings. Doubtless it hit the right note to gather in song during the nation's recovery.

By 1949, a first album had been released, and by 1960, the Krokodiloes had performed in sixty countries. The choral scene had become significantly more diverse since students sang in the university choir in the early 1800s. Other glee clubs—the Top Hats, Radcliffe Pitches, Kuumba Singers, Opportunes, Key Change and Din and Tonics—have been founded at Harvard. The Krokodiloes still sing their sparkling songs, and the group may be listened to on YouTube by all who appreciate the a capella tradition.

The Hasty Pudding clubhouse has moved several times. The Hasty Pudding Institute—comprising the Hasty Pudding Club, Hasty Pudding Theatricals and Harvard Krokodiloes—celebrated the unveiling of a new headquarters at the Hyde-Taylor House at 96 Winthrop Street in 2018. The "Kroks" took their name from the club room at Hasty Pudding, where they practiced when they coalesced in 1946, the room being furnished with stuffed crocodiles.

A hasty pudding was anything but hasty, as it took several hours to make. However, that was mostly boiling time, and the steps of combining ingredients were easy and couldn't go wrong. In New England, this familiar British dish was often called Indian pudding. The colonists called any dish with corn or cornmeal "Indian," and the white flour used in making pudding in England was replaced by the colonists with cornmeal. The people of Cambridge had kitchen gardens but were not farmers and bought the cornmeal from the indigenous people who lived outside their settlement. To the British recipe

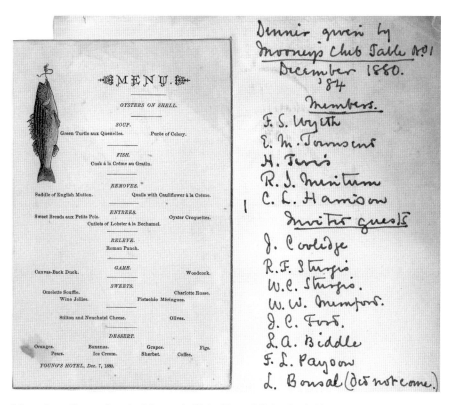

Menu from dinner given by Mooney's Club. *Harvard University Archives.*

they added molasses. A hasty pudding of cornmeal, milk, butter, eggs, molasses and spices is still served at every meeting of the club.

When the club was formed, the Wayside Inn in Sudbury, Massachusetts, was a tavern. Having opened in 1716, it has long been serving the classic dessert using the approximate recipe:

2 quarts milk
1½ cups cornmeal
2 cups molasses
Teaspoon each salt, nutmeg and cinnamon
⅓ teaspoon ginger
6 eggs

Boil the 2 quarts of milk in a heavy pan. Wisk in the cornmeal until thick. Add molasses, salt and spices and boil again. In a separate container, blend in the milk and eggs. Add the hot mixture to the cold. Bake in buttered and sugared casserole dish for an hour at 350 degrees. Note: It will still be wobbly when removed from the oven.

The Wayside Inn serves hasty pudding with whipped or ice cream.

Final Clubs

If a member of a certain Harvard final club had not earned his first $1 million by age thirty, the club would have given it to him—or so it was rumored. Being at Harvard already is being a member of a club. That identity etches deep or shallow, as the color crimson shades from deep pink to maroon in the décor of the Harvard Club of New York. Yet there are as many as thirteen clubs within the club, a surprise to many students and something of which townspeople who pass the clubs every day may be unaware. There are exclusive fraternities at other universities, but Harvard's final clubs are of the tony sort, conveying status in the manner of royalty.

The final clubs used to be so superior that a "scout" was sent out early in the evening to report back to members if a party was worth attending. They were established to give an experience of eating, dressing and play for the wealthiest students, who lived conveniently nearby in the "Gold Coast," three blocks of well-appointed residential halls bordering the Yard. As a refined touch, the Fox at 44 JFK Street has a fox head brass door knocker.

The oldest of the high-society clubs is the Porcellian. In 1784, a group of undergraduates got together for a dinner of roast suckling pig and all the trimmings. The group came to be called the Pig Club, later the Pork Club and at last the Porcellian, which survives on Massachusetts Avenue to this day. A number of the half dozen or so finals that remain were founded after Harvard College banned traditional fraternities in 1854. No such tie to a national organization had to be broken off for the Porcellian, which had been independent from the start. The Delphi derived from Delta Phi, which J.P. Morgan created because he didn't get into the club of his choice. At first to make its membership look larger, gas lamps were left lit by the front windows all night, resulting in its nickname "The Gas."

Ten to twenty students are chosen each year for each of the final clubs, several of which now include a few women. The exclusivity is at the heart of an off-quoted toast by John Collins Bossidy in 1910 at a Holy Cross alumni dinner. It goes as follows:

> *And this is good old Boston,*
> *The home of the bean and the cod,*
> *Where the Lowells talk only to the Cabots,*
> *And the Cabots talk only to God.*

Possibly the rest of the country is "town" for those who are caught up in Harvard prestige.

In the twentieth century, the social chasm between the scions of prestigious Boston, New York and Philadelphia families and everyone else was practically feudal. The richest students would not wish to fraternize with the middle class and poor students, and socially high-status people on the outside would equate the club a man had belonged to at Harvard as like a social register. Students lived in a very structured environment. As a member of the class of 1963 explained, "From Exeter 63 of us ended up at Harvard so we started out at college with a pretty large social network."

No wonder inequality was par for the course for Harvard's President Abbott Lawrence Lowell (1909–33), who mixed freshmen up in a freshman dorm before they joined houses for their second year but who, thumbs way down, excluded Black students from those dorms.

George Washington refused to be crowned king. Without Europe's royalty, the United States came to have other markers, especially money and prestige, to separate out the elite for a protected and exclusive life. While giving Kaiser Wilhelm a tour of the Harvard campus, Theodore Roosevelt announced the engagement of his daughter Alice to Congressman Nicholas Longworth. He pointed out to the kaiser that Nick and he both belonged to the Porcellian.

The Fly unanimously voted to include women yet changed their minds, favoring club unity, but the board intervened. A main activity of the final clubs is the selection of new members in the fall—the "punching season," consisting of cocktail parties, country outings and formal dinners attended by the "punches." There are club myths—for instance, that the Porcellian Club is so "old Boston" that its officers for each year are cousins.[3]

Theodore Roosevelt, Oliver Wendell Holmes and Justice Oliver Wendell Holmes Jr. belonged to the Porcellian. John F. Kennedy and Ted Kennedy were members of the Spee. Robert Benchley joined the D.U. It seems to have been a setback for Franklin Roosevelt when the Porcellian turned him down, but he made The Fly. "Legacies" whose fathers have given financial support have been favored. The clubs are keen on their traditions. In the late 1950s, there was apparently indignation when President Dwight D. Eisenhower was brought to the Porcellian as a guest, in violation of the club rule that no guest might visit the club more than once in his lifetime—Eisenhower had visited the club once before when he headed the Allied Forces.

A famous extracurricular Harvard club is the Hasty Pudding, not technically a final club because it admits students into its membership from all four years; it is a theatrical organization as well as a social club.

Two future famous journalists, Walter Lippman and John Reed, graduated in the class of 1910. Lippman cofounded a socialist club, and Reed while a member of Hasty Pudding leaned left. Their senior year, the student government election was a contest between the affluent students, who had servants in private apartments on Mount Auburn Street, and "the Yard," students of lesser means who lived in dormitories in Harvard Yard— Lippman captured most of the offices. Reed, despite being leftist, ended up aligning himself with the toffs. He was very ambitious to rise socially. Reed joined the Red Guards during the Russian revolution and became the subject of Warren Beatty's epic movie *Reds*.

Certain final clubs have amenities like a billiard table, library, sauna and squash court. In recent years, the college administration has come down sternly on the final clubs as anachronisms and bastions of snobbery in a university committed to diversity and openness. When campaigning for governor of Massachusetts, Deval Patrick resigned his membership of an all-male final club in 1983, seeing it as incompatible with his policies of inclusion. Senator Edward Kennedy likewise dropped out of The Owl—but not the Hasty Pudding.

An administrative initiative has declared that members of single-gender clubs would be stripped of on-campus leadership positions and could not be nominated for academic awards, including Rhodes scholarships, beginning with the class of 2021. It is a fluid situation at present. Despite the decades-long effort by the administration to get rid of the final clubs, the clubs themselves are waiting it out.

MURDER AT THE MEDICAL SCHOOL

Dr. George Parkman, a prominent doctor and businessman and a graduate of Harvard Medical School, disappeared in November 1849. The Charles River was dragged, and all the houses and outbuildings owned by Dr. Parkman in the West End of Boston were searched; handbills about Parkman's disappearance were distributed sixty miles beyond the Boston city limits.

It was a sensational case of murder in the medical school, as a week later Dr. Parkman's body parts were discovered in the coal burning stove, tea chest and privy of the medical school's dissection room. The school at that time (1847–83) was a modest building on North Grove Street close to the Charles. The remains were identified to be Parkman's because of the false teeth found in the stove and recognized by Dr. Keep, the dentist who had manufactured them for Dr. Parkman's lower jaw four years before. When Dr. Keep matched the cast of Parkman's jaw with the teeth recovered from the furnace, he wept.

Dr. Parkman was a person of high status, considerable fortune and property. Immigrants flooded Boston throughout the nineteenth century, and he was a major slum lord. This was the era when literary giants including Henry Wadsworth Longfellow, Oliver Wendell Holmes, Louis Agassiz, Charles Sumner, Asa Gray, Ralph Waldo Emerson and Nathaniel Hawthorne, the "Boston Olympians," met at the Old Corner Book Store and later at the Parker House. But Boston had its poverty-stricken immigrants from Europe living in miserable tenements. The potato famine in Ireland (1845–49), when the staple crop of Ireland was black and pest-ridden, had brought thirty-seven thousand Irish immigrants in but a few years. Some immigrants had experienced kind gestures from the doctor, medicine for their children and leniency about rent, while others cursed the ground he walked on. He was known to carry large amounts of cash with him as he went around collecting rent.

Suspicion fell on John White Webster, a quiet lecturer in chemistry at the medical school. He had a laboratory in the basement of the building where Parkman's remains were found. However, during the identification of the remains, Dr. Webster showed no signs of being perturbed. He was home for meals and at night with his family or visiting his neighbors with his wife and two daughters to play whist.

On the Tuesday before Thanksgiving, Webster delivered to the janitor of the Harvard Medical School, Ephraim Littlefield, an order for a Thanksgiving turkey. Was Webster ordering the bird for himself or giving it to the janitor who was an accomplice? No clue emerged.

Dr. Webster seems to have been a happy family man; however, he was in debt to Parkman and had an appointment to meet him on the day of Parkman's disappearance. According to the prosecution, Parkman had harassed Webster to pay him back.

The day after Thanksgiving, Littlefield borrowed the tools from a neighbor and broke through the walls of the vault below

Statue of George Parkman. *Harvard University Archives.*

Webster's chemistry lab, reporting that he saw on the basement floor parts of a dismembered body. He summoned the police, whose investigation uncovered a human thorax in a tea chest and false (mineral) teeth in the stove in Webster's office. These facts led to Webster's arrest.

Cartoonists far and wide had a field day drawing Parkman, a thin man, in his stovepipe hat, on his rounds to collect rents, and tens of thousands were drawn to the trial. Bleachers had to be put into the courthouse to accommodate those who had tickets, and the public had to be let in one group at a time. Curiously, the janitor reciprocated the holiday gift of a turkey by serving as the key witness for the prosecution.

There were irregularities in the conduct of the arrest and trial. After the inquest on December 13, the coroner's jury reported that Parkman was killed by Webster's hands, although Webster had not been at the inquest, and the witnesses had not been subject to cross-examination. Moreover, some claimed that the janitor who discovered the body had opportunity and motive (in reaction to how Parkman treated him).

The social circles of Dr. Parkman and Professor Webster overlapped. Initially shocked by the gory crime, people were then appalled when the quiet chemistry professor was accused. Fanny Longfellow, wife of the renowned poet Henry Wadsworth Longfellow, wrote:

> Boston is at this moment in sad suspense about the fate of poor Dr. Parkman. . . . You will see by the papers what dark horror overshadows us like an eclipse. Of course we cannot believe Dr. Webster guilty, bad as the evidence looks. . . . Many suspect the janitor, who is known to be a bad man and to have wished for the reward offered for Dr. Parkman's body. He could make things appear against the doctor, having bodies under his control. I trust our minds will be soon relieved, but, meanwhile, they are soiled by new details continually. I went to see poor Mrs. Webster on Saturday, the day after her husband's arrest, but of course was not admitted. What a terrible blight upon her life and that of the girls! The mere suspicion, for I cannot believe anything can be proved.[4]

Leave it to law school professors to turn the tragedy of the Parkmans and Websters into a matter of academic jurisprudence. At least through the twentieth century, the trial was studied at Harvard Law School because of the legal flaws in the proceedings.

Adjacent to the Massachusetts Statehouse are three row houses built on land once belonging to John Hancock. The central unit, 33 Beacon Street, was purchased in 1852 by Dr. Parkman's widow, who wished to lead a secluded life after the murder of her husband. It is now the official reception hall of Boston's mayor.

Henry Longfellow also attested in the trial to a strange occurrence one time when he went to dinner at the Websters' home. Dr. Webster had brought out a bowl of burning chemicals and turned down the gas lights. Forthwith he put a noose around his neck and dropped his head forward, tongue protruding, in an imitation of a man being hanged.

HENRY WADSWORTH LONGFELLOW

Joseph Roccasalvo, a polymath Buddhist scholar who was once a Catholic priest in Cambridge, is an American Romantic—that is, a Fireside Poet in Longfellow's tradition. In his poem "Memorable Silence," he wrote, "Be assured your everyday practice of generous love/ Heals the harsh memories you're so fearful of." They might have been the words of one of the American Romantics because they endeavored to communicate truth as well as beauty. The Fireside Poets, called that because their stirring rhyming cadences provided entertainment to a family at the hearth, have often been discounted as sentimental, yet a serious morality underlies their homely themes. British poetry had been America's idol, but in the latter half of the nineteenth century, a group of New England poets turned their sometimes flowery pens to the creation of lessons of moral guidance. The joys and traumas of Longfellow's life were etched particularly deeply. This master of metaphor poured his heart and experience into verse. He composed most of his poems at Cambridge—for instance, one dedicated "To the River Charles":

> *River! That in silence windest*
> *Through the meadows, bright and free,*
> *Till at length thy rest thou findest*
> *In the bosom of the sea!*
> *Four long years of mingled feelings,*
> *Half in rest, and half in strife,*
> *I have seen thy waters stealing*
> *Onward, like the stream of life.*

"Toiling,—rejoicing—sorrowing, Onward through life he goes;/ Each morning sees some task begun,/ Each evening sees it close." Henry Wadsworth Longfellow, the most revered American poet of his time, wrote these lines in "The Village Blacksmith" (1840). The blacksmith whom the poet so esteemed was Dexter Pratt at 54 Brattle, a house that from 1870 was for many years the home of the Walker family—Mary Walker was a woman who had escaped to freedom from servitude in North Carolina. Pratt forged iron parts for Nathaniel Wyeth, the Cambridge entrepreneur who invented techniques for harvesting and storing ice by machine.

Mary, Longfellow's first wife, died from complications of childbearing while they were traveling in Europe. He wooed and won his second wife, Fanny Appleton, a Beacon Hill socialite, some years later.

Portrait of H.W. Longfellow by Thomas Badger. Gift of Charles Eliot Norton, 1907. *President and Fellows of Harvard College.*

Longfellow loved European culture, but he needed a job. He shored up his fluency of French, German and Italian for two years. He aimed at a professorship at his alma mater, Bowdoin, but after teaching there seven years, he didn't get a promotion to a professorship, so he accepted the same post at Harvard. Longfellow was a fashion plate who liked his ruffled shirts and stylish clothes. Hiring him was an indication that Harvard aimed for worldly distinction in its faculty—being a training school for clergy was a dated role. Josiah Quincy III was president, and he said that the point of his college was to give students a "thorough drilling." The atmosphere was like an English boarding school. The lads were up a half hour before sunrise and went to service in an unheated chapel before breakfast. At a gong, it was lights out. The students pushed back with pranks—some involved concealing and lighting gunpowder in unoccupied spots. It was the last era when students were treated as schoolboys. Henry Thoreau (class of 1837) displeased the president by complaining of the arcane marking system by which marks for every recitation were given every day and infractions of the rules reduced them.

The bustle of the thickly settled center of town wasn't for Longfellow. He went for a walk one afternoon in May 1837 in search of a more secluded place, more conducive to study and poetry, and from which he could take a long walk to Mary's burial place at Mount Auburn Cemetery. Little did he know when he lifted the brass knocker of 105 Brattle Street a half a mile from the college, in the meadows by the Charles River, that he would live in the old Vassal mansion for the next forty-five years, first as a lodger taking two rooms and ultimately as the owner of the house.

The Vassall House, once for six months the headquarters of George Washington, was nicknamed "Castle Craigie" when Longfellow boarded there. It was the most impressive of the remaining colonial houses in town. It belonged to Elizabeth Craigie, widow of Andrew Craigie, the apothecary general of the northern department of the Revolutionary army appointed by Washington. After the Revolution, Craigie became a land speculator, especially in the watery landscape of marshes and mud flats of East Cambridge. The Craigies entertained the likes of Talleyrand and Queen Victoria's father, Prince Edward, in their home. The Craigies had ice all summer from their icehouse and flowers all winter from their greenhouse. However, Mr. Craigie fell on evil days. His large debts bankrupted him, and he never left his house for seven years except Sundays, for according to the law of the time criminals were secure on the Sabbath.

When Longfellow knocked on her door, the widow Craigie first turned him away. Her husband had left debts, but she, like many other Cambridge ladies after experience with Harvard students as lodgers, had decided not to let rooms to them anymore. He wasn't a student, Longfellow explained; he was a professor of the mature age of thirty and published. Mrs. Craigie, in her usual garb of slate dress and white turban, a cultivated reader of literature, drew back in surprise when she made the connection with the book on her bedtable that she was perusing before he entered. Longfellow was a great European traveler. Mrs. Craigie had her bookmark in a slender volume of his sketches of France, lying on her side table at that very moment.

Generations of Harvard students saw Mrs. Craigie sitting by her open window on a warm spring day, unperturbed by and oblivious to the fact that swarms of inchworms that infested the elm trees of Cambridge lay over her dress and turban. If Longfellow offered to remove them, she admonished him that an inchworm has a right to life as we do.

His notebook has an account of this visit:

The first time I was in Craigie House was on a beautiful afternoon in the year 1837. I came to see Mr. McLane, a law-student, who occupied the southeastern chamber. The window-blinds were closed, but through them came a pleasant breeze, and I could see the waters of the Charles gleaming in the meadows. McLane left Cambridge in August, and I took possession of his room, making use of it as a library or study, and having the adjoining chamber for my bedroom. At first Mrs. Craigie declined to let me have rooms. I remember how she looked as she stood, in her white turban, with her hands crossed behind her, snapping her gray eyes. She had resolved, she said, to take no more students into the house. But her manner changed when I told her who I was. She said that she had read "Outre-Mer," of which one number was lying on her side-board. She then took me all over the house and showed me every room in it, saying, as we went into each, that I could not have that one. She finally consented to my taking the rooms mentioned above, on condition that the door leading into the back entry should be locked on the outside.[5]

Longfellow was in mourning. He wrote to his friend George Washington Greene three months before the Craigie rooms were available, sharing his grief over his wife Mary's death:

In Cambridge, all is peace. Spring has come, bringing birds and blossoms....I take long, solitary walks, through the green fields and woodlands of this fair neighborhood. Yesterday I was at Mount Auburn, and saw my own grave dug; that is, my own tomb. I assure you, I looked quietly down into it without one feeling of dread. It is a beautiful spot, this Mount Auburn.[6]

By the end of the academic year, Longfellow was occupying a room in the colonial mansion. After three years, he added to his two upper rooms in the eastern side a third room in this suite. Then, after three more years, with his marriage to Fanny Appleton, he added half the house. Then, courtesy of a gift from Fanny's father, a wealthy man on Beacon Hill, Boston, they occupied nearly the whole house. Longfellow rarely left home again after his marriage to Fanny, as they raised a family of six children. Ms. Craigie continued to live there, in two rooms of the house reached by a landing approached by a staircase at the rear of the house, and beyond her in the ell lived a farmer whose wife cooked for Mrs. Craigie and Longfellow before his marriage (he said she scolded him and overcharged him for the two meals she prepared for him).

Longfellow wrote a friend shortly after moving in, "I live in a great house which looks like an Italian villa....Have two large rooms opening into each other. They were once General Washington's chambers."[7] He and most

Longfellow House, residence of H.W. Longfellow. *Art Resource.*

of the other American Romantic poets of his generation were situated in the Northeast. They composed poems as the conflict intensified during the antislavery movement. Their poems offered comfort that the backbone of the country was strong. Longfellow kept to traditional verse forms and imbued his poems with moral guidance. He also took on the themes of the injury Europeans wrought on Native American culture in *The Song of Hiawatha* and of the persecution of the Acadian French during the French and Indian War in *Evangeline*.

Longfellow shunned public speaking. At age forty-seven, in 1854, he gave a final lecture after eighteen years as a Harvard professor. The subject was Dante's *Inferno*, and he vowed that it would be the last lecture he would deliver at Harvard or anywhere else.

Many of Longfellow's poems were quiet and meditative. This is the mood in which Longfellow rendered his impression of his blacksmith neighbor into a poem that generations of schoolchildren memorized. Longfellow was a Fireside Poet who extracted lessons about living from rural New England life, as did Thomas Cole and Alfred Bierstadt in their American landscapes. Why write if not teach how to live?

The poet's son Charles rebelled against the cozy lifestyle he could have had. Like his father, he was interested in the world outside the familiar and was a tireless international traveler. While Charles inherited land on the south side of Brattle Street (two of the ten lots partitioned from Henry

Skating club. A field at the corner of 40 Willard and Mount Auburn Streets was flooded to make the pond, and a skating club was formed in December 1897. The land was a gift from one of H.W. Longfellow's daughters, Annie L. Thorp. The club thrives today. *History Cambridge.*

Rindge and the drying sheds in view behind the pond, undated. *History Cambridge.*

Longfellow's estate among his five surviving Longfellow children in 1882), he did not build on it. The long lot across Brattle Street was donated to the City of Cambridge to become Longfellow Park.

It wasn't long ago that a typical evening's entertainment in middle-class American homes combined singing early American folk songs accompanied by piano and poetry reading. The point of *Evangeline* was to reflect in a hushed and prayerful mood on the deportation of the Acadians from Nova Scotia, like some of my family.

Henry and Fanny Longfellow were seldom apart. He said it was part of their theory of life, never to be separated. When Fanny was invited to a ball, she proclaimed she preferred their fireside readings. They loved raising their children, and their help included a cook, maid, nanny, gardener and coachman. For seventeen years, the couple's cup ran over with marital bliss, until the summer of 1861, when on one hot July day tragedy struck. Fanny was on a terrace on the east side of the house with Edie, age seven, and Annie, five. The mother was sitting at a long carved Italian table overlooking the east of the house. She wore a light muslin summer dress. She had snipped a lock of Edie's golden hair and put it into an envelope as a keepsake. Then she took melted candlewax from a burning candle for sealant. Something must have knocked over the candlestick, and a sudden breeze ignited the wax. She ran to her husband's study, where he was napping. They held each other, and he threw a small rug over her. His hands became very burned, and the flames encompassed her. She died unconscious and peaceful in the morning. The funeral was held on July 13, 1861, which would have been their eighteenth anniversary.

Such fatal accidents were not uncommon. Dancers died in their flimsy dresses from the gas footlights, and the open-weave fabric of crinolines, as Mrs. Longfellow wore that day, were highly flammable. Fire retardant was already in use for Queen Victoria. One month after Fanny's tragic end, there was published the segment of *Great Expectations* in which old Miss Havisham burns alive in a wedding dress she had worn ever since her wedding was canceled.

The "Village Blacksmith" begins, "Under a spreading chestnut-tree." The horse chestnut stood in front of Pratt's house on Brattle Street until it was cut down when the street was widened in 1876. Money was raised by Cambridge schoolchildren for a chair that was constructed from the chestnut's wood and presented to Longfellow on his seventy-second birthday. The poet composed an affecting poem "To the Children of Cambridge" on the occasion:

> *Am I a king, that I should call my own this splendid ebon throne? Or by what reason, or what right divine, Can I proclaim it mine? Only, perhaps, by right divine of song It may to me belong: Only because the spreading chestnut tree Of old was sung by me.…And thus, dear children, have ye made for me This day a Jubilee, And to my more than three score years and ten Brought back my youth again.*

A plaque commemorates the site where the tree once stood, and the fancily carved Gothic chair can be seen in the study at the Longfellow House.

Longfellow wrote expressively how he kept his boyish lilt through the tragedies that beset him, comparing himself to the Endecott Pear tree, planted by an early governor of the Massachusetts Colony. Today, an eleventh-generation Harvard College graduate, an attorney who bears the name of that Puritan soul, comes to visit and pay tribute to the ancient tree, noting that his primary admiration is for the tree, not the Puritan. John Endecott's eldest son, John, had no children, so descendants of the longtime governor of the Bay Colony trace their ancestry back to the ten children of a second son, Zerubbabel, a colonial surgeon.

ARNOLD ARBORETUM

Of Harvard's wealth of museums of art, science and history, only one is free to the general public. This is the Arnold Arboretum, 281 acres of trees in Boston's Jamaica Plain neighborhood, on the grounds once belonging to the indigenous Massachusetts tribe from which the Commonwealth took its name. This 1872 joint venture of the university with the City of Boston is part of the "Emerald Necklace" of parks and parkways that Frederick Law Olmsted laid out for the Boston Parks Department after he had completed a similarly naturalistic design for New York's Central Park. Much more than a park, it is an educational institution with vast laboratories, library and archives available to scholars from around the world. The Arboretum offers all kinds of classes for children and adults, tours and exhibitions. It has served the mission of research and advancing the world's knowledge of the plant kingdom for more than 150 years.

The land for the Arboretum was left by James Arnold, a whaling merchant from New Bedford, and the endowment to Harvard came from Benjamin Bussey, a Boston merchant and experimental farmer who raised the food for his lavish entertainment on his estate. Harvard was to supply the plants and Boston the maintenance; the Arboretum was given a one-thousand-year renewable lease. The university appointed Charles S. Sargent (class of 1862), former major in the Union army, as director, a post he held for fifty-four years.

It took Sargent years of diplomacy to persuade the university and Boston to join to create the Arboretum. Harvard agreed to give the land and make it open to the public, and the city agreed to pay for the infrastructure.

A brilliant collaboration occurred between the tireless horticulturalist Sargent and the social reformer Olmsted, driven to create urban parks where poor and rich could meet and mingle. At times they clashed; Professor E. Beveridge, advisor for the Olmsted Park restoration projects, recounted one such occasion.

Olmsted left for a European trip before planting began in spring 1892. A few days after his departure, Sargent descended on the firm's office, commandeered the planting list from Olmsted's nephew and adopted son John and deleted most of the foreign plants, as well as numerous other trees and shrubs that he disliked. In all he excised one-third of the trees on the list and a quarter of the shrubs. When John objected, Sargent threatened to terminate the Olmsted firm's connection with the Brookline Park Commission. While no such dramatic rift took place, Sargent had his way.

View of the Boston skyline from atop Peters Hill. *Rose Lincoln, Arnold Arboretum.*

He ordered the plants he wanted and saw that they were planted. Among them were only two foreign species: Japanese barberry (*Berberis thunbergia*) and the European brier rose (*Rosa eglanteria*).

Sargent was a conservationist who worked with John Muir to preserve America's wilderness, and the mission of the Arboretum has always had two important prongs: as a park to the citizens and as a scientific research center.

To celebrate the 150th anniversary of the Arboretum, three dawn redwoods were planted at Elmwood, the current Harvard president's off-campus house. The previous president's abode was on campus at 17 Quincy Street, which can be rented for functions; before that, the "Old President's House" was the president's residence from 1850 to 1920.

The dawn redwoods growing at Elmwood are deciduous conifers smaller than the other two species of redwoods, growing to seventy-five or one hundred feet, that used to be common in North America. Without the discovery of a small grove of the species in Szechuan Province, the tree would likely be extinct. In 1941, Harvard sent an expedition to China to locate the trees. The members of the expedition collected and sent back four pounds of the seeds. Dawn redwoods lose their coppery leaves in the winter. The Elmwood trees were propagated from hardwood cuttings taken from the Arboretum's oldest example.

The idea of a living museum of trees goes back to ancient Egypt. To beautify her palace and boost her eternal renown, Queen Hatshepsut, who ruled during the fifteenth century BC, launched an expedition to Punt ("God's land") in northeast Africa for resinous trees. Archaeology suggests that frankincense and other precious trees were brought back in reed baskets and planted in circles around pools at her temple at Deir el Bahri on the west side of the Nile opposite Luxor.

While European royal gardeners focused on flowers, André Le Notre loved his bosquets and *allees* and only planted flowers at the king's insistence. Many botanists were sent to America; for instance, a botanist who served the Sun King's grandson Louis XVI discovered a purple rhododendron in the Blue Ridge Mountains. The tradition continued in force at the Arboretum: the scented Katsura pods came in an envelope from Japan and propagated a tree now one hundred years old at the Arboretum. Plant explorer E.H. Wilson brought back from a decade of travels in East Asia more than two thousand new plants and observed that many North American species, like the tulip tree, had affinities suggesting an Asian origin. On his Asian travels, he would stay in one city and go out on long travels in a sedan chair. He nearly died in an avalanche but was rescued by his Chinese botanists. Wilson made exquisite glass plate photographs of New England trees in the 1920s. Seeds were also sent by interchange with scientific institutions and gardens abroad.

Because of its unusual connection with a city and a university, the Arboretum is an exceptional trove of knowledge of its plants—records of fifteen thousand accessioned plants georeferenced on map layers to begin with, available to scientists around the world. A new plan due to threats to the diversity of plant populations caused by climate change involves expeditions throughout the northern hemisphere to sample plants in the wild. Meanwhile, there are lectures, guided walks, school programs and weekly e-mails and posts to Facebook by the director, Ned Friedman, an evolutionary biologist, highlighting marvels at the Arboretum. For instance, he has studied specimens of *Franklinia*, which grow on Bussey Hill and are among the most sensitive plants in the Explorer's Garden. The plant has an unusual pattern of a seven-month dormancy in the winter between pollination in late summer and the development of first fruits the next spring. Friedman speculates that the long waiting period for bearing fruit evolved as the plant's subtropical ancestors migrated north and adapted to colder conditions.

The Arboretum in springtime. *Arnold Arboretum.*

ROMANTICISM IN ARCHITECTURE

A diversity of buildings typifies an old college campus. Across from two of Harvard's eye-catching modernist buildings, the School of Design and Gund Hall, is a building in a very different, Romantic style, Sever Hall. But Sever Hall, dating from the late 1870s, isn't everyone's tankard of grog. The stone exterior is grim and the brickwork dull. Nevertheless, it witnessed an era. The classrooms used to be so dark that students blinked to stave off sleep—despite one wall of each classroom painted a lighter color to try to counter the effect and draw students' attention to the instructor. H.H. Richardson built it after Trinity Church in Boston, which has a light-filled interior, and before his Shingle style, exemplified by the Stoughton House at 90 Brattle Street.

The law school was luckier with his later work. The façade of Austin Hall at the edge of Harvard Law School on Massachusetts Avenue is interesting and original. It is admirable that the first floor comprises three huge classrooms to go with new teaching theories about the law. I acknowledge

Austin Hall circa 1882–93. *Charles Sullivan Collection of Harvard Photographs, Cambridge Historical Commission.*

the imposing qualities of these buildings—the heavy stone walls and Syrian arches, the carved and molded brickwork and the bulging towers that only go half-round. My widowed grandmother, an impoverished schoolteacher, and her two children lived in the turret of just such an edifice, although the faux-Gothic style was not named Richardson Romanesque. An Austrian princess who fled Continental Europe in the 1860s when the Prussians won territories found a New York City architect who built this for her— massive stone walls, faux turrets and an arched porte-cochere—reviving the glory of her ancient medieval family and which might have served as King Richard of England's prison. The children had to tiptoe down the stairs from the turret so as not to disturb the princess. They escaped the fortress when my grandmother married the superintendent of schools and moved into his house, an Arts and Crafts bungalow.

Richardson or his collaborator Augustus Saint-Gaudens's idea of decoration can be discerned by the forty-two portrait busts of Julius Caesar that were removed from Sever Hall during a renovation. Among the wooden benches in the dark halls, one had an incised checkerboard, and another had a crucifix scene with saints. Again, many praise these buildings, and Richardson was clearly an innovator. Earlier he built the beautiful Trinity Church (with Arts and Crafts interior) in Back Bay, Boston. Richardson's Sever Hall was a Teutonic Carcassonne breaking with the tradition of Federal and Georgian buildings at Harvard, known as the "Harvard style."

Austin Hall's exterior is faced with sandstone in polychromic patterns. The light stones form a checkerboard. The central entryway is framed with a triple arch of sandstone, placed deep in the building. The decoration is chivalric. The reading room has an ornamental fireplace and beams carved with the heads of dragons and boars.

Regarding Harvard's eclectic and harmonious architecture, by great architects like Josep Sert and Walter Gropius, the most wonderful part is how the paths of Harvard Yard and beyond crisscross, so people meet one another and sense the travails and the excitement of learning face to face. Pick your favorite building. Mine is the University Hall by Charles Bullfinch, elegant white granite, dating from 1812.

ENCOUNTERING WILLIAM JAMES

Orbiting around the two great universities are centers and institutes that engage the town and gown in dialogue. On the outside, they look like many of the charming residences of Cambridge, except that plaques identify them as housing the study of an area or question of thought like intellectual moons. Nestled in the leafy border of Old Cambridge across from the Harvard Divinity School is one landmark attempt at combined colloquy with community that was something avant-garde in appearance and purpose from 1957 to 2003.

The experiment was twofold, bringing together scholars from many religions and cultures and providing rooms for course study and events. Thirteen bachelor apartments faced Francis Avenue, with a central garden. Students and Harvard affiliates might apply, and etiquette meant that a big poster of Marilyn Monroe mounted in a front window by a graduate student's desk had to be taken down.

Just a few blocks away from this experiment of housing with seminar rooms was the house that William James built in 1889 and occupied with his family. His father, Henry James Sr., was a theologian, and his house was at 20 Quincy Street.

Despite a highly irregular education at multiple institutions in the United States and Europe, James was a major figure at Harvard for forty years. His career, however, was as irregular as his education. In the 1860s, while a student in Harvard's medical college, he assisted Louis Agassiz at the Museum of Comparative Zoology. Agassiz embraced a ghastly eugenicist theory that extended the idea of selective breeding from animals to humans. He was Harvard's most famous scientist, though, and James sailed with him to Brazil, where the biologist conducted fieldwork intended to refute the upstart Charles Darwin. In 1870, now with a medical degree, James taught the first psychology course at an American university. Throughout most of his Harvard career, he was a member of the philosophy department. At 95 Irving Street, William James hosted students. He taught many who later became famous. A favorite was Gertrude Stein. On the day of the exam, Gertrude showed up and told James that she did not feel like taking an exam. James told her that was all right, as he often felt that way himself. James reveled in his library with its twenty-two-by-twenty-seven-foot area with floor-to-ceiling bookcases, preserved through renovations of the house. In the basement, young scientists raised rabbits and chickens for animal intelligence studies. James caused a nationwide stir by shunting attention away from

Center for the Study of World Religions, 42 Francis Avenue. *Cambridge Historical Commission, staff photographer.*

theology to vivid individual experiences, including the paranormal, which he felt gave clear evidence of humanity's innate religiousness.

In 1957, a few blocks from James's house, the Center for the Study of World Religions became a physical reality. Funds came from an anonymous "Little Lady"—this is how her Harvard beneficiaries referred to her to ensure anonymity—who aimed to bequeath her considerable estate to a university that would create a program to study "the great religions of the world." Krister Stendal, dean of the Harvard Divinity School, set aside an acre of his residential lot, and Josep Lluís Sert, dean of the School of Design, who had studied architecture in Barcelona before coming to New York, a modernist par excellence, built a three-sided, two-story building with housing, offices, a common room and residences looking out on a central courtyard. Wags in the Yard, a mile from Frances Avenue, referred to the Center as "God's motel." James was a forebear of the unorthodox center because he took the plurality of religions as a fact rather than an aberration from central revelation.

The Center became an exemplar of what Harvard had prided itself on since the nineteenth century: world rank, including eccentrics and even renegades, seeding the highest intellectual exchange. There was a spy for a distant regime, a venerated scholar who admitted privately to having made his living as a young man smuggling opium, linguists of the sort who would add on to their linguistic repertoire an Algonquian language or Provençal for fun and heads of universities in their own countries. A few bright young recent college graduates were tossed in for local color. There was also an Iranian Sufi who routinely played his soulful violin on the flat roof and sat on the floor on a carpet inside a tower of his stacked books, as well as a blind Shi'a-born Lebanese Christian who also played the violin and the tabla in a rock band. Learned and witty Jesuits joined the center in the mid-'60s, and the bagpipers at one of John Kenneth Galbraith's parties could be heard from the Center's inner courtyard. Mingling may be the secret of great universities.

On an upper floor of William James Hall were once super-intelligent rats that for generations had been working the mazes to test various behavioral theories. Although the Hall was named for him, William James never embraced the kind of controlled experiments that came to dominate the discipline in his later years. He exclusively studied people and coined the word *multiverse* in 1895 to mean the mystical inner labyrinth of worlds in the heart and mind of a human. He and his wife, Alice, tried to communicate with their deceased infant son, Herman, through a trance medium named Leonora Piper. In addition to his personal motivation to bridge the loss of a child, James was a founding member of the American Society of Psychical Research. Before he died, he promised Alice that he would be in touch after death. However, she never reported such an event.

William's younger brother, Henry, the Nobel Prize–winning novelist, is revealed through the fictional characters he set in motion. While he became a British citizen in 1915, he had deep ties to Cambridge. His last novel, *The Bostonian*, is set in the aftermath of the Civil War. A southern gentleman, Basil Ransom, James's alter ego, goes to Boston and becomes embroiled with feminists who try his patience. One of the young women is mocked for responding to the flirtations of Harvard students. Ransom tours Harvard and is impressed by Memorial Hall, which he compares to the halls of Oxford: "It arched over friends as well as enemies, the victims of defeat as well as the sons of triumph."

Henry, William and the rest of the James immediate family are buried in the same plot at Cambridge Cemetery on Meadow Avenue across the street from Mount Auburn Cemetery. Six headstones stand in front of an oblong red-brick wall.

Civil War

The corps of Cambridge volunteers in the war began to form when James P. Richardson, an attorney with offices in Central Square, proposed in the *Cambridge Chronicle* to organize a company to defend the Union. Any citizens of moral character and sound body were invited to call at his office. By the spring of 1862, one hundred men had enlisted in Company D, 5th Regiment of the Massachusetts Infantry. This unit fought at Gettysburg and other battles. This was just one of the regiments where Harvard students, alumni and faculty obtained commissions. Oliver Wendell Holmes (class of 1829's class poet) had been living at home when he enlisted in his senior year. Serving three years in the 20th Massachusetts Volunteers, he rose to the rank of lieutenant colonel. The number of deaths from combat or war-related disease would be the equivalent of two average class years.

The names of the soldiers and sailors and the battles in which they died are inscribed inside Memorial Hall, and at the east end of Annenberg Hall are painted replicas of regimental flags, the original flags being fragile and stored for safekeeping. A monument at the middle of the sixteen-acre Common flanking Harvard Square pays tribute to the 939 men from Cambridge who died in the war. A soldier stands at the summit of the sculpture, and Lincoln is in a niche formed of arches below.

The 20th Massachusetts Volunteer Regiment was called the "Harvard Regiment" because so many Harvard faculty and students fought in it. It is estimated that of seven hundred soldiers on the first train of Union army volunteers, just forty-four would survive the war. I am reminded of my father's 1940 class at Annapolis, which saw the most casualties for the same reason, that they served from the beginning of a war. However, whereas my father and his classmates were united in their beliefs as to why they fought for their country, at Harvard there were many southern secessionists. Between 1855 and 1861, sixty-seven southerners were admitted as undergraduates. Some may have been Unionists, but someone scribbled an angry note of "Nole within" on the May 1861 cover of the *Crimson* and returned his copy. (*Nole* is the imperative singular of the Latin verb *nolo*, literally "do not wish it"—in brief, "don't.")

Also, factions volunteered who were patriots but also non-abolitionists who had sympathies with the South. It was rumored that "secessionists" among the law students were going to attack the arsenal on April 29, 1861, and armed students and faculty organized to guard it overnight.

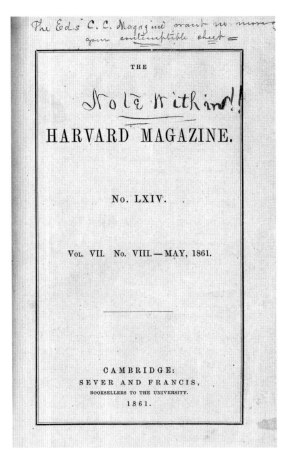

Left: Civil War cover of *Harvard Magazine*, May 1861. "Nole within." *Harvard University Archives.*

Below: "Class Day at Harvard," from *Ballou's Pictorial Drawing-Room Companion,* July 3, 1858, wood engraving by Winslow Homer. *Ray Austrian Collection, Harvard Art Museum/Art Resource.*

In November of that year, sixteen teenage girls met at the house of the eminent botanist Asa Gray and founded a social club to provide clothes and bandages for the Massachusetts forces. The club was originally called the Banks Brigade after Nathaniel P. Banks, who led the state's forces at the onset of war. Later the name was changed to The Bee, which continued work in the First World War and on behalf of the Cambridge Hospital until disbanded in 1931.

Knowing the terrible progress of war, it is painful to read how innocently soldiering began. Recalled by a citizen of Cambridge, it sounds like a Winslow Homer scene, yet Homer painted many Civil War scenes that are far from as lighthearted as the painting I have in mind.

In the Civil War, of course, the arsenal was guarded. Students were excused from recitation to form the "Arsenal Guard," and some of the children were afraid to go to the end of Follen Street because, inside the high fence, a sentry in blue coat, with musket on shoulder, walked up and down. The small boys were, on the contrary, much attracted. George Saunders, who lived on the corner opposite the arsenal, was one of many who marched beside the student companies as they came up from college to relieve the Home Guard. When he carried over cookies and doughnuts, he was told he had saved the men's lives and to go home again and ask his mother to send more. His little brother, who was very engaging, was called the "Child of the Regiment."[8]

Robert Todd Lincoln (class of 1864) did not go to the front, as his mother did not allow it. He had been rejected from Harvard on his first application, but his father had him do a finishing year at prep school and he was admitted on a second try. A curiosity is that he received demerits for smoking. After graduation, he went to the Harvard Law School, where he argued court cases with students including Oliver Wendell Holmes, who took a seat on the Supreme Court at sixty-one and served for close to thirty years. Holmes had been wounded three times but nevertheless found his experience most meaningful. In an address he gave in 1895 called "The Soldier's Faith," he wrote that the war was "horrible and dull but its message was divine."[9]

A May 1861 *Harvard Magazine* was returned by a Southern student who said that the editors of his Confederate magazine "want no more of your contemptible cheek."[10] The cover is shown on page 120. Inside is tipped in a letter from an anonymous reader in Kentucky, a portion of which reads "as your ably conducted '<u>Magazine</u>' has been transmogrified into a <u>one-horse</u> <u>political circular</u>, and as you advocate a policy obnoxious to every young man and citizen of the South—probably you had better keep it at home and send it to your <u>roguish abolition brethren</u>."

The Bee, "Workers in Four Wars." *History Cambridge.*

During the war, those who remained students at Harvard were sheltered. They and those who had served and come back, many wounded, to conclude their studies only wanted to get on with life. The Baccalaureate Sermon, Oration and Poem of the class of 1865 by John Quincy Adams Brackett, who would become the thirty-eighth governor of Massachusetts, did not whisper of the Civil War. "No Lethean stream shall ever obliterate" the scenes of their college life, he proclaimed. "Although we shall know them in reality no more, they will ever be among the brightest, most lasting gems in the casket of remembrance."[11] Brackett concluded by enjoining his classmates to "go forth to meet the shadowy Future, without fear and with manly hearts." This oblique reference to the war was one that was required for men who fought in it.

WILLIAM RANDOLPH HEARST

Students drop out from lack of money, to join the armed forces or because they are too much in a rush to enter a larger sphere to stop at "Go" and collect a diploma. One year after Theodore Roosevelt (class of 1881), a student serious about his studies with an accent on mathematics, graduated, William Hearst (class of 1886) arrived as a freshman with a much lighter, satirical attitude. He gave big beer parties and bought the first "Sanctum" for the *Lampoon* editors on Mount Auburn Street between Dunster and Holyoke Streets, using his own funds. Hearst was a member of the A.D. Final Club, Hasty Pudding Theatricals and the *Lampoon*. He stayed three years, during which time he transformed the *Lampoon* to a paying enterprise with exciting news and big headlines as its business editor. A tall, well-dressed student known for crossing campus smoking long cigars, he often was at the center of misadventures. A sensationalist prank was to have a gift delivered to each of several professors of a chamber pot with the professor's face drawn in the bowl. Hearst also kept a pet alligator while at Harvard. After three years, for one caper too many, Hearst was expelled. He returned to California and made a success of his father's struggling newspaper, the *San Francisco Examiner*, as its publisher while his father went into politics. By his thirties, Hearst was a media tycoon. He also became the toast of Hollywood with his mistress, the actress Marion Davies. They entertained lavishly at his hillside estate in San Simeon. Hearst's yellow journalism drew the United States into the Spanish-American War, while his advocacy of isolationism did not convince Americans to stay out of World War I. In 1950, Hearst ordered his publications to kill a story of the *Lampoon*'s being confiscated as pornography by the Cambridge District Court.

HOWE, MANNING & ALMY

The lives of the 150 women who have been nominated to the Cambridge Women's Heritage Project span more than four hundred years. Marieke Van Damme, the director of History Cambridge, said that she would be curious whom I selected to write about—no wonder considering how fascinating they are, from Louise Frances (Jones) Barlow, a former slave; to Mary W. Baines, a Cambridge pilot for thirty-five years; to Marilyn and Sheila Shelman, the "Brass Sisters," local cooking celebrities. I chose Lois Lilley Howe (1864–1964) because her story exemplifies that an American university town gave women a chance to flourish in their métiers in the twentieth century when career opportunities were still limited.

Lois Lilley Howe grew up at 1 Oxford Street, now the location of the Harvard Science Center, in a fine house with a cow in the field. In girlhood, she was fascinated by the building of Memorial Hall on Kirkland Street close to the Howe home. Workmen nicknamed her the "little superintendent" because of her interest in construction.

The Howes belonged to the Cambridge intelligentsia. They were abolitionists and active in other causes of their times. Tragedy, however, assailed the family. Lois lost her elder brother, aunt and uncle while young. Her father, Ester Howe, a physician, owed his prosperity to the gas light business. The introduction of electric lighting severely reduced his fortune, and he died in 1887. Mrs. Howe downsized, and Lois, who had graduated from Cambridge High School, had to sell the house. The new owner wanted to remodel the straight staircase, and Howe devised a solution even after the owner's brother-in-law, the prominent Boston architect Robert Swain Peabody, said it was impossible to change the stairs.

The move turned out to precipitate Lois's career, even though she had initially been discouraged from it. She wrote in her recollections for her fiftieth class reunion in 1940, "Always interested in houses, I had wanted to be an architect but had been suppressed by my pastors and masters on the ground that I could not be an architect because I was a woman."[12] However, MIT was made a land grant school by the Merrill Act of 1862, resulting in its admitting women long before other Massachusetts colleges did (the land grant schools were bound to do so). Her MIT graduating class was two women and sixty-four men. Encouraged by Peabody to enter a competition for the Women's Building at the Columbia Exhibition in Chicago, she won a second prize for her design. The first prize winner was also an MIT graduate, Sophia Hayden, who was from a four-year program, while Lois was from a two-year program. The award money for the prize Lois received took her and her mother and sister to Europe for eighteen months. Soon after they returned, Lois received her first commission, to design a house for a recently married friend.

Pioneering Women of American Architecture describes Howe's struggles during her first years as a professional architect; she may have had to supplement her income with other employment. Her specialty, not uncommon for women in the early twentieth century, was always residential work. She designed dozens of houses, the documented number being 426 projects, so that she influenced the look of Cambridge over her forty years of practice (Howe lived to one hundred). Works by her firm, Howe, Manning & Almy, can be seen on the website of the Cambridge Historical Commission.

The commissions Howe got were for domestic architecture. Revivalist styles were in vogue, and she studied the Colonial and Georgian examples in New England, taking photographs and measuring features, some of which were published in *Details from Old New England Houses* (1913). Howe designed carriage houses, barns and homes in Cambridge. She focused on decorative detail inside, while the outside was plain—comfort and utility, fitting with tradition. She devised porticos, moldings and fireplaces for each house. Howe was the first woman elected to the American Institute of Architects. The recognition was even more significant given that women were not allowed to be members of the Boston Society of Architects.

Howe brought into her practice first one and then another partner. Her first partner, Eleanor Manning, originally from Chicago, graduated from MIT in 1913. Her interest was more modest homes and housing complexes. At this time, the United States had three other firms founded and run by women, the most notable being the San Francisco firm of Julia Morgan, established in 1904, which designed William Randolph Hearst's San Simeon and carried out the reconstruction of the Fairmont Hotel after the 1906 earthquake.

In 1926, Mary Almy was asked to join the thriving firm. She graduated from Radcliffe and MIT and came from an old Cambridge family, giving her connections that brought numerous commissions. One was for Mary's younger brother, Charles, and another for her parents. The Charles Almy Jr. House at 147 Brattle Street (1926) became for a time the home of Governor Joseph B. Ely.

E.E. Cummings

The lauded twentieth-century poet E.E. Cummings was a consummate insider when it came to Cambridge. His father, Edward E. Cummings, was a Harvard professor and pastor. The parents moved into their new Colonial Revival house built in 1863 at 104 Irving Street, north of Kirkland Street on the woodsy backside of Cambridge, across from William James and his family. The commodious three-story clapboard house with thirteen fireplaces was theirs to prepare for having a family and had enough space in its triangular front yard for a touch-football game. E.E. Cummings was born the next year. His mother dressed him in a white sweater on which she had embroidered a crimson *H*. The future poet's parents were liberal Unitarians. They sent him to the Agassiz School, a public school near Harvard with a predominantly white faculty and student body and whose principal was Maria Louise Baldwin, a graduate from Rindge High school and a teacher training school in Cambridge. Baldwin was a civic leader and innovative educator at a period when "African Americans found acceptance at Harvard and success at the ballot box—a progressive trend that was reversed in the 20th century."[13] This included a few Black men on the Board of Aldermen, in the common council and in the legislature. William H. Lewis, a graduate of Harvard Law School, coached football at Harvard for twelve years before being appointed assistant attorney general in the Justice Department in 1911 by President Taft.

The Agassiz School was renamed the Maria L. Baldwin School in 2004. From E.E. Cummings's book *six lectures*:

> *Miss Baldwin, the dark lady mentioned in my first nonlecture (and a lady if ever a lady existed) was blessed with a delicious voice, charming manners, and a deep understanding of children. Never did any demidivine dictator more gracefully and easily rule a more unruly and less graceful populace. Her very presence emanated an honour and a glory: the honour of spiritual freedom—not mere freedom from—and the glory of being, not (like most extant mortals) really undead but actually alive. From her I marvellingly learned that the truest power is gentleness.*[14]

William James had the informal role of the poet's godfather. He had introduced the couple. Edward was a colleague, and Rebecca was a psychology researcher. Today, Irving Street is an inner part of Cambridge, but in 1889, the James house had been the first dwelling in the neighborhood. E.E. Cummings lived in it until his death in 1910, calling it his Elysium; until 1968, his grandchildren still occupied the house.

Cummings lived at 104 Irving while an undergraduate at Harvard and while completing degrees in art (BA, 1915; MA, 1917). During his freshman year, while still living at home, he had written a paean to the university and the city, writing, "I am of the aristocracy of this earth. All the advantages that any boy should have are in my hands. I am a king over my opportunities." As a senior, he had a liberated and wild period where he frequented strip clubs and burlesque theaters in Boston. After receiving his master's, he worked as a printer in a New York bookstore. He was an ambulance driver in France during the First World War and then lived in Europe.

Number 104 Irving was a typical Cambridge-style solidly constructed mansion. Mr. and Mrs. Cummings wanted their children to have healthy outdoor fun, therefore the house had swings and a sandbox. There were apple trees in the oval front lawn, which was ringed with a white pine hedge.

Being an insider, Cummings could be trenchant in his description of Cambridge's well-bred university community. In one poem, he mocked

Cambridge ladies, who were educated and had connections to Harvard, as "furnished souls." They valued old-fashioned poetry over his (verse that rejected formal grammar and spelling). He worked into his poems how they knitted for charity while gossiping about scandals and were unbeautiful and had comfortable minds:

> *(also with the church's protestant blessings*
> *Daughters, unscented shapeless spirited)*
> *They believe in Christ and Longfellow, both dead,*
> *are invariably interested in so many things—*
> *at the present writing one still finds*
> *delightful fingers knitting for the is it Poles?*
> *perhaps. While permanent faces coyly bandy*
> *scandal of Mrs. N and Professor D*
> *…the Cambridge ladies do not care, above*
> *Cambridge if sometimes in its box of*
> *Sky lavender and cornerless, the*
> *Moon rattles like a fragment of angry candy*

The Maria Baldwin House is now a National Historical Landmark at 196 Prospect Street, the northern half of a nineteenth-century duplex.

PHILLIPS BROOKS HOUSE

Phillips Brooks was a pastor of South Church in Boston who had a powerful and kind personality. He was descended from an old North Andover family—there are many Brookses in the state's history. He and his younger siblings spent their summers at North Andover in a capacious 1752 house still there, inheriting it in 1881. He graduated from Harvard in 1855. Brooks had a habit of suddenly bowing his head and making a spontaneous prayer. He was six-foot-four and weighed three hundred pounds, talked fast and delivered his sermons so rapidly they could hardly be understood. Yet his words aroused spirit and affection. John F. Kennedy has been quoted for repeating a familiar line from a Phillips Brooks sermon: "Do not pray for easy lives. Pray to be stronger men!"

Brooks composed poetry, hymns and the lyrics to "O Little Town of Bethlehem." His eloquence was remarkable. In 1880, he preached in

Westminster Abbey and at the Royal Chapel at Windsor to Queen Victoria. He was a friend of the architect H.H Richardson and designed Trinity Church with Richardson when he was a rector of the church.

The day of his funeral, his casket was carried by Harvard students for miles from Trinity Church in Boston, across the Charles River, through Harvard Yard and west to Mount Auburn Cemetery. The *Crimson* published an anonymous proposal by an alumnus to build a social service house in his honor, and plans were quickly underway.

The Phillips Brooks House was dedicated and transferred to Harvard on January 24, 1900. It was intended as a gathering place for all the religious societies, and it was dedicated to piety, hospitality and charity. Since that time, students have become more involved in public service. Harvard has conducted hundreds of community service programs in the Boston area and beyond. During World Wars I and II, it hosted the ROTC, Red Cross and Cambridge Draft Boards.

It has been estimated by the university that two in three Harvard students do volunteer work in Cambridge now. The first time a Harvard student pointed out to me the Phillips Brooks building, I asked whether we could

Phillips Brooks House, March 1962. *Bertram Adams, Cambridge Historical Commission.*

Harvard Glee Club, 1920s. *Harvard University Library.*

go in. The tradition was established not to make a fuss or broadcast the organization's good works, services such as mentoring for area youth, literacy training and counseling at summer camps. Kids on the Common doing athletics with a Harvard student, or being tutored, is a mingling of town and gown without precedent in town and gown's early history.

Part IV

MODERN TIMES

C ambridge has faced off with Harvard, David against Goliath, over property during the last century—see treatises by Charles Sullivan, authority on the history of the city's real estate. When nostalgia for college days is shaken off, it is clear that it is more for youth than any place or institution, yet sometimes the two converge. In the 1970s, the youthful population of Cambridge zipped around its leafy streets, in the present divided into residential districts so nobody can park anywhere but in front of his/her own house, and it is hard to watch movies from *The Trial of the Chicago 7* to *Love Story*, as they bring back difficult memories because the director got it right.

CAMBRIDGE BRAHMANS: THE DANAS

An endemic aspect of town and gown was the prominent families. In the nineteenth century, the Danas, descended from a Puritan patriarch, were Cambridge's most prominent family. Francis Dana (1743–1811, Harvard class of 1762) fought in the Revolution, became a delegate to the Continental Congress from 1776 to 1789 and helped reorganize George Washington's army at Valley Forge. When Francis Dana served as American minister to Russia from 1781 to 1783, his secretary was John Quincy Adams, future U.S. president, who named his son Charles Francis Adams in his former chief's honor. The ambitions and patriotic services of the Adams and Dana families were connected for generations.

Francis Dana had numerous children and owned a great deal of property in the east of Cambridge, where he encouraged his children to settle. His daughter Martha married the distinguished artist Washington Allston, while he and Richard Henry Dana (RHD Sr.), her brother, became immersed in Gothic novels and found inspiration in Samuel Coleridge, whom Allston had met in Rome in 1806. They found Harvard stodgy. After RHD Sr. was expelled, along with sixteen other fellows, for participating in the food protest known as the Rotten Cabbage Rebellion in 1807, he was off to Europe with Allston.

Richard Henry Dana Jr. (1815–1882), or II, received his undergraduate degree in 1835 and his LLD in 1866. His rebellion was more far-reaching than his father's,

Breakfast menu, Memorial Hall, Thursday, November 10, 1904. *Harvard University Archives.*

and he was the most famous exemplar of the Dana tribe in the nineteenth century. In his junior year, worsening vision called him to put books aside and take a two-year sea voyage, enlisting not as a gentleman but as a merchant seaman. In the summer of 1834, RHD II left Boston on the brig *Pilgrim,* bound for the west coast of North America by a route around Cape Horn. The memoir he wrote would attract great attention. As he stated in the preface, the book was a true narrative of an unprecedented genre:

> *The change from the tight dress coat, silk cap, and kid gloves of an undergraduate at Cambridge to the loose duck trousers, checked shirt, and tarpaulin hat of a sailor, though somewhat of a transformation, was soon made, and I supposed hat I should pass very well for a jack tar. But it is impossible to deceive the practiced eye in these matters and while I supposed myself to be looking as salt as Neptune himself, I was no doubt known for a landsman by everyone on board as soon as I hove in sight.*[1]

The first boat to come alongside when the sails were finally furled in Boston Harbor was a pleasure boat belonging to the junior partner of the

Richard H. Dana Jr., 1891–1900 print of an original photograph dated around 1849 of Dana at age thirty-four. *National Park Service, Longfellow House, Washington Headquarters National Historic Site.*

firm that owned it, an acquaintance of Dana's. This person jumped on board, shook the captain's hand and inquired of the mate for Dana, whom he congratulated on his brave adventure. How reduced his status had been at sea, Dana would stress in his memoir:

> *The last time I had seen him I was in the uniform of an undergraduate at Harvard College, and now, to his astonishment, there came down from aloft a "rough-alley" looking fellow, with duck trousers and red shirt, long hair, and face burnt black as an Indian's.*[2]

Dana's account also described the coast of California, as well as the storms of an Antarctic winter when he raced up and down the ice-clad riggings to furl and unfurl the sails. Herman Melville, in chapter 24 of *White Jacket*, wrote, "If you want the best idea of Cape Horn, get my friend Dana's unmatchable *Two Years Before the Mast*. But you can read, and so you must read it. His chapters describing Cape Horn must have been written with an icicle."

After seeing the sadistic practices of Captain Thomas, the captain of the ship on which Dana sailed, which included flogging, Dana vowed that he would help the lot of the common seaman. Having returned to Cambridge, he attended Harvard Law School. An abolitionist, he helped found the Free Soil Party to prevent the expansion of slavery into the West. He went on to specialize in maritime law, especially defending seamen and runaway slaves in court. He wrote a handbook called *The Seaman's Friend* (1841), which became a reference on the legal rights and responsibilities of sailors. In 1854, Dana, as a rising lawyer, was walking by a Boston courthouse where a crowd had gathered. Inside, a twenty-year-old runaway named Anthony Burns was being tried. Burns had stowed away in a ship in Virginia and was working in Boston when he was arrested for a spurious jewelry store theft and imprisoned. There were arrests of abolitionists who rioted in protest of Burns's arrest, and the state militia was brought in. Dana II represented Burns. Although Burns was transported back to Virginia, the owner (under pressure) was paid $1,300 to free him. Ironically, Judge Edward G. Loring— who had taken the high road and ruled, despite his personal beliefs, that Burns had to return to slavery—found himself fired from a post at Harvard. Burns's freedom was celebrated publicly in Boston; he went on to theological studies and became a minister in St. Catharines, Ontario.

Dana (RHD II) during the Civil War successfully argued before the Supreme Court an important case, that President Lincoln had the power under the Constitution to blockade Confederate ports.

Richard Henry Dana III (1851–1931), son of RHD Jr., of *Two Years Before the Mast* fame, grew up on Berkeley Street with the future ornithologist William Brewster and the sculptor Daniel Chester French, his childhood friends. At Harvard, he captained the varsity crew, and he graduated from Harvard Law School in 1877. RHD III married Edith Longfellow the next year. He served on commissions that oversaw the building of the Charles River Dam and Longfellow Bridge and was the trustee of organizations including the Episcopal Theological School and the Cambridge Boat Club. Richard and Edith's son, Henry Wadsworth Longfellow Dana, received a doctorate in philosophy from Harvard in 1910. Columbia University dismissed him in 1917 for pacifist activities. He returned to live at the Longfellow House and became a supporter of progressive causes. He visited the Soviet Union numerous times between 1927 and 1935. He collected family archives, made the Longfellow House (once George Washington's headquarters) a repository and wrote *Three Centuries of the Danas in Cambridge* (1941).

RHD III came down to New York to attend the christening of his grandson, Richard deRham. The grandfather confided, looking at the child in the cradle, that the baby possessed "the back of an oarsman."[3]

"THE FRUITFUL INVASION"

The scholar Charles Eliot Norton (class of 1846) reminisced in 1897 on Old Cambridge in his childhood, when it was the country (not in the heart of a city):

> *But even a greater change than that from country village to suburban town has taken place here in Old Cambridge in the last seventy years. The people have changed. In my boyhood the population was practically all of New England origin, and in large proportion Cambridge-born, and inheritors of Old Cambridge traditions. The fruitful invasion of barbarians had not begun. The foreign-born people could be counted up on the fingers. There was Rule, the excellent Scotch gardener…there was Sweetman, the one Irish day-laborer…ready to lean on his spade and put the troublesome schoolboy to a test on the Odes of Horace or even on the Arma virumque cano [from Virgil's Aeneid]; and at the heart of the village was the hair-cutter Marcus Reamie, from some unknown*

135

Cambridge Fire Department, Engine no. 6 (unit in front of truck and station, River Street near Howard), now Rindge School of Technical Arts, 1921. *David T. Dickinson Jr., History Cambridge.*

"Little France," North Cambridge Club. *History Cambridge.*

foreign land, with his shop full, in a boy's eyes, of treasures, some of them brought from distant romantic parts of the world by his sailor son. There were doubtless other foreigners, but I do not recall them, except a few teachers of language in the College.[4]

Old Cambridge, as the kernel of the town was known, can be thought of as evidencing little change as the waves of immigrants evolved the city. Central Square became a large commercial center, with East Cambridge the industrial hub (where charming Colonial Revival details like Doric capitals and fluted columns are still very visible). In 1846, Cambridgeport, East and North Cambridge and Old Cambridge joined to form the city. Immigrants resided and to a large extent worked outside the purlieus of the Harvard nexus in these neighborhoods.

Skilled laborers from as far as Germany, Labrador, Nova Scotia and the British Isles manned the early industries. After the Civil War, the Black population tripled, many coming from Nova Scotia and the West Indies, as well as the Great Migration to the northern states. Irish came when grain prices plummeted back home and they couldn't pay the English landlords the rent, and again during the potato famine, with many settling in North Cambridge. Portuguese, Swedes, Italians, refugees from the Russian empire, Greeks, Syrians and Armenians were among other immigrant groups who arrived from 1890 through the Progressive era, seeking a viable new life. The Irish would be the first immigrant group to get political power. Typical of U.S. cities, Cambridge and Boston had a reputation for embracing newcomers, but also typical of U.S. cities, the reality was complex, with church-related tensions often running high. In 1834, an Ursuline Convent in Somerville was sacked by a mob.[5]

But the settlement houses and central and branch libraries of Boston and Cambridge made a concerted effort to support the schools with homework help, a warm place to go and in cultivating in children the literature of civilized democracy. It had to gratify an adult who contributed to the progressive agenda to hear a little girl say, "I always think of Proserpina going back to King Pluto, when I go down to the subway." Applying to be a page at the Boston Public Library, boys were asked to name a great general, a great philosopher and a literary name of antiquity. While Harvard continued to produce patricians, the lives of the inhabitants who were immigrants seem to have been difficult but vibrant and full of promise, as today.

North Cambridge had clay beds worked by the New England Brick Company from 1844 until World War II. This pit was allowed to fill with water by 1870 and became a swimming place, though not without risk. The pit was named after Jeremiah McCrehan, who came from Ireland, worked on bridges and started a brick works. He lived in a neighborhood called "Dublin" at 146 Rindge Avenue.

Why Lowell's Portrait Does Not Hang in Lowell House

The first public speech of John F. Kennedy was for a speech class he took in his third year at Harvard. He was twenty, and he raised a biographical fact regarding FDR's appointment of Hugo Black, an Alabama senator, to the Supreme Court in 1937: Justice Black, who during his time on the Supreme Court became a supporter of civil rights legislation, had been a member of the Ku Klux Klan as a young man. Kennedy (probably in Holden Chapel) spoke with gravity and modesty. It is his first speech ever recorded, and it can be freely listened to today.

A repellant piece of American history overlapped town and gown, with Cambridge being both more realistic about the danger of the Ku Klux Klan and more open in resistance to it than Harvard, at two moments when the Klan was drumming up members, in the '20s and the '50s.

The Klan was active in Cambridge and solicited members from the Harvard student body in 1923 and 1924. Born in the atmosphere of hate in the defeated South in the Reconstruction era, the Klan had a second burst of influence in the 1920s; in a wave of anti-foreign hostilities, membership soared in New England. The Harvard chapter was founded in about 1921, when the Klan played on the fear of immigrants and Catholics as well as of people of color.

In April 1923, a gathering of 150 women members of the Knights of Columbus Auxiliary took place. Before piano solos and singing, in a hall decorated with American and Irish flags and buntings, Reverend James Kelly "spoke on the un-American spirit of organizations like the Ku Klux Klan."

Irene Linda Gordon, professor emerita of history at New York University and author of *The Second Coming of the KKK*, observed that numerous universities had chapters of the Klan:

KKK chapters appeared at many northern universities in the 1920s. The students faced no economic threats, but in general the attraction of this Klan seems to have had little to do with economic motives—people raged against Jews, for example, without ever having met a Jew. We see today how hysterical, violent anger can be created by demagogues.[6]

After the release of D.W. Griffith's hugely popular racist movie *Birth of a Nation* in 1915, racists saw an opportunity to spread hate. The Klan reformed in Georgia along the lines of a nativist ideology, featuring the costume and flaming crosses that may have originated in the movie. The foremost perceived new enemies were immigrants, especially in the Northeast; Irish Catholics; and French Canadians. Cambridge had Klan branches at that time as well.

A 2021 article in the *Crimson* traces Klan activity at the university in the early and mid-twentieth century. That included two KKK meetings in North Cambridge in October 1923: "Students switched to the 'intellectual' Brookline, Mass Klan chapter after becoming disillusioned with Cambridge. Harvard Klansmen thought the Cambridge chapter was controlled by 'low-brows.'"[7]

Some years ago, a photograph was uncovered in the Boston Public Library archives of Klanners posed in their garb for a graduation photo on Class Day 1924. They were gathered at the foot of John Harvard's statue in Harvard Yard, spooky and scary in their Klan garb of white robes and peaked hats, the robes neatly hemmed at the bottoms and at the cuffs. The Klansmen wear neat trousers and dress shoes. One of them holds a boater, preppy attire, in his hand.

The repudiation of the Klan by the Masons was in Cambridge newspapers over the first half of 1923. As opposed to opinion pieces, there were reports on events in town, like a party for a new dental office at which a member of the clergy made a stirring address denouncing the KKK and calling for freedom of worship as guaranteed under the Constitution. A notice was sent to all the Masons warning that no Freemason could be a Klansman and vice versa. Frederick W. Hamilton, the fourth president of Tufts and a Mason, commented in Masonic papers, "The Klan calls itself an invisible empire. There is no place for an invisible empire in the United States. Masonry stands four-square for the United States and its constitutional principles and usages."[8]

In the city of Cambridge, there was awareness, concern and condemnation from the pulpit and the Masons. There were many new immigrants, especially

Irish, one ethnicity targeted by the Klan. The Klan as a danger was discussed and denounced. By contrast, Harvard's official policy, endorsed by President Lowell, was to tolerate the presence of the Klan.

A notice was issued by the Faculty Deans in the spring of 2019:

> *Lowell's tenure as University President—which stretched from 1909 to 1933—was marked both by the major changes he instituted at Harvard and by his racism, homophobia, anti-Semitism, and xenophobia...students should not have to see images of the two Lowells—after whose family the House is named—in such a prominent space.*

During his tenure, Lowell created the house system and worked to integrate students from different socioeconomic backgrounds. He also tried to cap the number of Jewish students at Harvard and excluded African American students from living in Harvard Yard. Alongside former dean of the college Chester N. Greenough (class of 1898), he led a purge of gay students—the "Secret Court" of 1920—apparently connected to at least one suicide.

In 1953, a cross was set afire at midnight in the corner of campus where students of color had their rooms. An architect of the class of 1955, J. Max Bond Jr., was among fifteen Black students and would recall that the cross burning was declared a prank and that Black students were told that they would be expelled if they did not agree to the hush-up. Bond insisted that it was not a prank. A semblance of a happy ending occurred when Lowell House, named after President Lowell, was renovated. When the House reopened in the fall of 2019, the portraits of Lowell and his wife, Anna Parker Lowell, were not displayed in the dining room.

RADIO SCHOOL

Sometimes when we dash across Harvard Yard as a shortcut to wherever, we might think about the young men who were minted there not with a bachelor's degree but a radio operator's certificate in Morse code and mechanics, knowledge gained as quickly as possible before they were sent into war.

A few months after war against Germany was declared (April 1917), the U.S. Naval Radio School was launched by Harvard and the U.S. government (officially offered by the university to the navy). War makes situations for

"R.A. Emery in front of our mansion, 31 Everett St., Cambridge, Mass. 3/25/1918" (written on reverse of photo). *Cambridge Historical Commission, Harvard Radio School Collection.*

sacrifice and bonding together, and in this case, Harvard and Cambridge worked together in an extraordinary way. Shortly after the radio school opened, Harvard became the place to go for telegraphics, and other such schools were closed.

It was foreseen that many more people skilled in Morse code would be needed, so the U.S. Naval Radio School was launched by Harvard and the U.S. government in the very month that war was declared. For the rest of the war, it occupied nine Harvard campus buildings for instruction. Recruits who reached an aptitude of ten words per minute were drawn from Naval Reserve stations around the country and sent to Harvard. Upon reaching twenty-two words per minute, the recruit graduated and was transferred to the fleet. By the armistice, there were 3,480 men under instruction by around 75 instructors; they were demobilized in early 1918. Austin Hall (the law school) was used for classes for 600 men at one time. The young men were complimented by the Cambridge chief of police for their good behavior, and they were invited to parties and picnics. Sleeping quarters were in the gymnasium, and barracks were put up in Harvard yard. Some of the men boarded with Cambridge families. Sometimes there were two shifts of classes from early morning to night, although after a new school building was opened on the Commons, the school went back to the single shift. Military drill was given for an hour and forty-five minutes six days a week.

From the *Cambridge Chronicle*:

> *The people living or doing business in and near Harvard square certainly are aware that there is a war. Radio boys are everywhere, and the daily parades through the street in the vicinity sometimes led by the ROTC band and at other times by a drum corps, force one to stop and take notice. The square has really taken on the appearance of a naval cantonment, although it is not so apparent as it will be when the barracks are erected on the common for the reason that the boys for the most part are now housed in the college buildings. The presence of the radio school has made business in the square much more brisk than ever before, and the merchants are catering to their needs in every direction possible, and the result of their trade is very perceptible. One effect of the coming of the Radio boys has been to somewhat change the character of the square. The former staid and dignified appearance of the locality has certainly departed and more of a commercial and cosmopolitan aspect is apparent. The change is very noticeable. It is seen even in the outward appearance of the buildings, one illustration in particular being the transformation of a section of the block next to Brock Brothers' store which has been painted white to advertise a sanitary barber who has been located on the second floor. If this sort of thing continues Revere beach and Bass Point will "have nothing" on Harvard square.*[9]

There were the familiar town and gown questionings, however. Some were concerned that the Cambridge misses were stepping out with the radio school students. A state senator was up in arms that a tree might be felled to make space for the radio school. These matters were discussed in newsprint, between the patriots and those concerned. A few days before construction was started in early June 1918, William Crane, the contractor in charge, reassured the public that not only would the trees be left undisturbed, but the sidewalks would also be built over rather than dug up. The article in the *Cambridge Chronicle* was headlined "Trees on Common Not to Be Molested."[10]

PROTESTS

Students for a Democratic Society (SDS) began as a civil rights movement at the University of Michigan in 1959. It shifted focus to opposing the Vietnam War in the mid-1960s and led antiwar protests in many universities. A dramatic incident occurred at Harvard in November 1966 when Secretary of Defense Robert McNamara was attempting to leave campus and was prevented from doing so; hoisted up on the hood of his convertible, he agreed to answer questions from the crowd about the Vietnam War. The next October, a recruitment taking place on campus by Dow Chemical, which supplied napalm to the military and in which Harvard had significant stock, was interrupted by protests. A student who was at the Divinity School, Michael Punzak, later a public school teacher and prominent music educator in Cambridge, was in and around the steps by the John Harvard statue where the action occurred:

> *Harvard at some point gave us the choice of being arrested or turning over our bursar's cards. My friend was SDS but he didn't want to be arrested and neither did I. We gave our bursar's cards and left wondering if we would be expelled. To our surprise the Harvard Divinity School gave us back the cards immediately—with a letter of congratulations for sitting down for our principles.*[11]

Another time when the administration sided with the students was two hundred years before, in July 1768, when the patronage of American manufacturing was made the test of patriotism. Graduating Harvard students came to commencement dressed in clothes of American manufacture and were permitted by the governor to appear in them.

On the night of April 8, 1970, representatives of SDS (three hundred students) tacked a list of demands to the door of the office of Harvard's president, Nathan Pusey. The central demands targeted the Reserve Officers' Training Corps (ROTC), which SDS wanted removed from campus. Participants in the ROTC program received a paid college education in exchange for committing to serve in the military after graduation. The faculty wished to reduce the presence of ROTC, but the Harvard Corporation refused to terminate the program. President Pusey rejected all the demands—abolishing ROTC being the foremost.

While students at Boston University made their point by occupying a building in protest, Harvard students staged a takeover of University Hall, a major administration building in Harvard Yard. Administrative staff mostly left the building peacefully, although some were forcefully expelled. One of the most prominent Black administrators at the college, Dean of Students Archie Epps III, resisted the takeover and was physically carried out of the

Protest in Cambridge. *Spencer Grant Collection, Boston Public Library.*

building. There were about five hundred students inside University Hall that morning. But a protest that was meant to be a nonviolent sit-in escalated. Police assembled and stormed up the steps into the hall. About seventy-five students and police were injured. Many of the students were charged with criminal trespass at the Cambridge District Court. Next students assembled at Memorial Hall and called for a three-day strike.

The District Court levied a fine on 170 of 174 participants in the takeover. On the administration's side, a "Committee of 15" (which included 5 students) handed down disciplinary action, including the expulsion of 23 students, who could reapply to return, and 3 more who were permanently expelled; 2 students spent nine months in jail for assault and battery, but the dramatic occupation reaped results. In its aftermath, ROTC lost its privileges, and student representatives were given a role in choosing faculty for the new department of African American studies.

It was impressive to be among a crowd of thousands at the rallies at Harvard Stadium during the week following the strike. Many of our generation did not trust the changing internal leadership/radicalization of SDS. Students and faculty were joined in the judgment that the war was pointless, a terrible model for foreign policy. And underlying politics was social upheaval, a cultural battle between the establishment and the yippies. A local mother was acting dean of admissions of Radcliffe at the height of the protests. Her son recalled, "She had files from her office she brought home every day in a banker box."

The student movement went beyond the antiwar movement. The more moderate group that emerged from SDS's Harvard chapter combined an antiwar rally with protest of the trial of Black Panther leader Bobby Seale. They got legal permission to march on April 15, 1970, a day selected to highlight tax money going to the war. About 1,500 demonstrators split off from a massive peace rally at the Boston Common and, led by the November Action Coalition and including members of women's liberation groups and Youth Against War and Fascism, marched from the Boston Common to Harvard Square. Rioters threw bricks; smashed windows of the Northeast Federal Savings Bank, Holyoke Center and the Coop; threw a firebrand through the Coop's front window; looted Saks Fifth Avenue and Bobbi Baker; and gutted two police cars with fire. At eight o'clock, the police started charging the protesters with tear gas.

The Associated Press reported that about 300 protesters and 35 police had been injured; 120 of them were treated at Stillman Infirmary and the Old Cambridge Baptist Church. Harvard maintained that few Harvard students were involved and that any students arrested would receive legal assistance from the university. About 30 demonstrators were arrested.

At the 1970 commencement, SDS would have interrupted the platform during the exercises, but senior class officers persuaded Pusey to allow a five-minute statement by SDS members. Pusey in the annual report described it as a "dismal year." The criticism of the administration of many colleges like Harvard eventually led to giving students and faculty more of a voice in governance, curriculum and community relations.

Future Supreme Court justice Clarence Thomas was at the protest. A student at the College of Holy Cross in Worcester, where he started the Black Students Union, he had been a political activist who protested the war in Vietnam until the April 15 event. In his memoir, *My Grandfather's Son* (2008), he wrote how the turn of the demonstration to rioting "horrified" him, disillusioned him about current student leftist movements and initiated his conservative ideology:

> *It was intoxicating to act upon one's rage, to wear it on one's shoulder, to be defined by it. Yet, ultimately, it was destructive, and I knew it.*
>
> *So, in the spring of 1970, in a nihilistic fog, I prayed that I'd be relieved of the anger and the animosity that ate my soul. I did not want to hate any more, and I had to stop before it totally consumed me. I had to make a fundamental choice. Do I believe in the principles of this country or not? After much angst, I concluded that I did.*[12]

REVERBERATIONS

The other half of the demands of the Harvard affiliates who occupied University Hall in 1970 related to the community, and this became a long-term cause of negotiations for food service workers and guards as well. Strikers in the Boston/Cambridge area in 2002 wanted wage increases for workers.

Five thousand students, workers and others from the community protested low janitorial wages in a rally on February 26, 2016, involving civil disobedience. The protest began in Harvard Square, crossed Massachusetts Avenue and circled Harvard Yard. The protest action was coordinated in advance with the Cambridge Police. Nine protesters, members of Harvard's Progressive Student Labor Movement, blocked traffic by creating a line holding hands and were arrested.

Sunrise on Memorial Drive, Cambridge. *Spencer Grant Collection, Boston Public Library.*
Spencer Grant graduated in journalism from Boston University and worked as a freelance photographer from the 1960s until the mid-1980s in Boston, for magazines and services, among them U.P. International, the *Boston Globe* and *TIME* magazine. His photographs are in the collections of the Boston Public Library and Tufts University.

Several dozen students picked Harvard's oldest surviving building, the red-brick early Georgian Massachusetts Hall, as the locus to protest the low wages paid to janitorial, food service and maintenance workers. The hourly wage was slightly increased. Harvard established a contract in February. To carry this progress to the rest of the Boston area, students and janitors marched through downtown Boston on October 1 as two thousand workers of the same union that represents Boston and Harvard janitors went on strike, their aim being medical benefits for part-time workers and higher wages. Three Harvard undergraduates and one Harvard Divinity School student were arrested at the Prudential Center and charged with disrupting the peace and trespassing.

In the wake of the building occupation, a group at Harvard Divinity School was founded called Equitas to work for peace and justice. They supported the living wage campaign as well as the wider janitors' strike. In Boston, a civil disobedience action at the Prudential Center preceded the 2002 janitors' strike. The charges were eventually dropped because the security footage of the action clearly showed that they were never asked to leave (thus not trespassing) and were not disorderly.

The result of the activism is that in the ensuing years, the pressure on Harvard for higher wages for these workers has resulted in much better pay. Of course, university expansion is one reason why many had to commute from far away on unreliable public transportation for the good steady jobs. By 1970, Harvard and Radcliffe owned about 120 residential properties bought and earmarked for development since 1953, and Harvard was planning several high-rise projects. In *Building Old Cambridge*, it is noted that "in 1956 City Councillor Alfred Vellucci repeated the old threat to set Harvard off as a state of its own like the Vatican." In 1970, residents of the Riverside neighborhood occupied commencement. The university set a temporary moratorium on land acquisition in 1972. The issue of university expansion took an interesting turn when the plan was proposed for a Kennedy library in Cambridge: "In Old Cambridge, opponents of the proposed Kennedy Library were accused of disrespect toward the late president."[13] JFK had originally chosen to have it located next to Harvard. The community feared traffic congestion, and so the plan was abandoned in 1978 for an oceanfront site next to U Mass Boston. The library was designed by I.M. Pei, as Mrs. Kennedy wished.

Meanwhile, affordable housing has continued to be the biggest issue in Cambridge in modern history. There was rent control introduced from 1970 to 1995, since which cooperation between the city and the university has had planners and architects from Harvard and MIT staffing the Community Development Department and grown strategy has focused on the periphery of the city, balancing economic development with affordable housing and transportation.

PRANKS AND CAPERS

MITers share with many other engineering minds a finesse, or gift. One of my sons-in-law smiles and says that his grad studies at the Institute were easy. At MIT Labs, my son, a scientist, who keeps his mind busy during long drives by solving math problems, thinks that his work is as fun as soccer. We suspect that despite how smart they are MITers sometimes work night and day—the mascot of the Institute is a beaver. But there is a strong association of their work to play. According to Institute historian T.F. Peterson in *Nightwork: A History of Hacks and Pranks at MIT*, the hack, or prank, is judged "by how elegantly it accomplishes its purpose."[14]

The standard of a hack is that the people who create it are anonymous, and it does not leave a disfiguring mark on the environment. Ideally, it is a public event, often seen as awesome by everyone in the locality or, in the case of hacks at the Yale-Harvard game, irritating to the other university down Mass. Ave. Iconic hacks have featured one of the huge domes or a huge interior building, as when MIT students have made a large object appear in an inaccessible place, like putting a campus police cruiser or a telephone booth on the Dome. It is fine if there is a trick of the eye, a travesty of the object.

There have been many fraternity hacks at colleges. An MIT hack seems to be at a whole different level in the way of technological finesse.

The first hacking group on record was the Dorm Goblin, which threaded a thirty-five-foot telephone pole through one dorm and took a live cow to the roof of another. The ideal hack defies expectations, like a dorm room set up on the Charles River. The term in the 1960s meant doing something unexpected, which broadened to cover mischievous ventures of no practical nature that tested the skill, wit and imagination of the hackers. According to Mr. Peterson, the term was first used in print in the 1970s.

Early on, automobiles were often a prop. Hackers impaled a Ford coupe high up on a building. In the picture of the hack by the Dorm Goblin, where a Ford chassis was hauled up five stories of the East Campus Dormitory and perched with its wheels over the side, the student pictured in the driver's seat was James Kilian (class of 1926), MIT president from 1949 to 1959.

The two signature domes have been "popular venues for hackers' surrealist dioramas," wrote Peterson. Legendary is the simulacrum of a police car on the 100-foot-wide Great Dome (Building 10). A sign on the back window read, "I brake for donuts." The dome has had a 9-foot candle on it for MIT's 100th birthday. On Halloween in 1962, it became a Great Pumpkin, covered with orange mesh. In 1987, a papier-mâché snowman was erected on the 115-foot high Small Dome, on the Rogers Building, and in 2001, a snowman made of real snow was placed there. In 2019, when the movie *Avengers: Endgame* was released, the Great Dome was redecorated as "Captain America's shield."

Another locus of hacks is the Green Building, as when its twenty-three stories are turned into a message board. Cambridge and Boston have taken note when the lights on the windows spelled out "11" to honor the Apollo 11 mission to the moon of Neil Armstrong and Buzz Aldrin, MIT class of 1961. On the Academy Awards night when *Good Will Hunting* was nominated for nine awards and won two, an image of Oscar feted the

Musician cab driver. *Spencer Grant Collection, Boston Public Library.*

Good Will Hunting, with Ben Affleck and Matt Damon, 1997. *Bridgeman Images.*

film. The movie's star, Matt Damon, was born in Cambridge, although he and Ben Affleck met in a neighborhood in Newton where Affleck grew up. Hackers in 1998 drew attention to tuition inflation with a banner "Welcome MIT Debtors."

There are street signs as well, like "Go Slow Geeks Crossing Ahead" or over a door "Tropic of Calculus," and a weather balloon emblazoned "MIT" was inflated at the Harvard-Yale football game in 1982. The renowned sculptor Daniel Chester French, who dropped out of MIT in the late 1860s, unable to handle the math, created the design for the bronze statue of John Harvard in Harvard Yard. This has been hacked over the years, by the rules, doing no harm.

On the tradition of student hacks, John Durant, the MIT Museum director, stated:

> The saying "Tech is hell" expresses that this culture you are in causes you to have a very hard time. Pressure often causes a push back, which formulated as hacking. A hack is a practical joke played on the institution, a student culture passed down, anonymous, often secret, funny, and not meant to do the world harm. Oliver Smoot was a student in the '60s. Students measured

Harvard Bridge (the bridge from MIT to Boston) taking Oliver Smoot as the unit. A joke is how many smoots to the moon. There is a ruler of Smoots, i.e., smoot stick. At the museum Mr. Smoot was measured again in about 2010 and he had shrunk, calling into question his use as a ruler.[15]

At the MIT Museum, where there had been a whole gallery of hacks, now they are dispersed throughout the collection.

Professor Andre De Hon of the University of Pennsylvania was at MIT from 1986 to 1996. He has observed,

MIT hackers learn to envision new things. They learn management, delegation, teamwork, planning, failure analysis, and public relations.... They learn that they can turn their own visions into reality, and they learn how to do it. It's hard to imagine a more valuable tradition for an institution like MIT. The fact that this tradition was not handed down by the faculty or administration but evolved among the students and continues to thrive is indicative of the special environment that is MIT.[16]

The hacks also entertain the Institute and the community at large. It is fascinating to think how invention and joyfulness go together. The MIT Museum, which opened in October 2022, has examples of many useless theories that became advances for humankind. Claude Shannon's Theseus, an intriguing early computer, has a magnetized mouse that can change its objective, explore a maze and register the new path. The mouse not only follows an algorithm but also remembers. A "deep fake" shows how there were two speeches ready for the Apollo moon landing, in preparation for success or failure. "Corry's Yellow Chair" by Arthur Ganson and Andy Cavatorta has a miniature chair whose pieces come together and then, over and over, separate into places on a star formation. That section of the exhibition is called Totally Useless Things, but so were the extraordinary inventions on display in early stages. And most playful of all may be a small, quiet object, a plate-sized silver-coated silicon wafer, shaped at nano scale, that was created as a monument to the MIT community. The image appears as the MIT seal, but if magnified sufficiently, its "atomically" smart, smooth face is a mosaic of the names of nearly every student, professor, administrator, custodian and lab assistant who has been part of MIT from 1871 to 2020.

If MIT pranksters tend to stellar IQ inventiveness as they learn to envision new things, Harvard in a mood to prank has looked outward and often to arch-football rival Yale. Folk and blues singer Tom Rush, Harvard class of

1963, who was making music in coffeehouses in the Square by night and taking classes in the Yard in the day, recalled:

> *One fall Yale welded the gates to all of Harvard shut. In retaliation, the Harvard students came down to New Haven in a truck and dug a trench across one of the major streets on the campus. They put up the little smudge pots that construction people used to put up so that people could see there was something going on. While the group were working, New Haven police came over to direct traffic around them. Then the Harvard guys left and people wondered when they were coming back. Several days went by and people realized they weren't coming back.*[17]

Scuffles are inveterate and presumably in police reports. Charlie Merrill (class of 1968) recalled one time, after there were muggings at Longfellow Bridge, when Harvard students set up a trap, sending a small slender student across and waiting for him to be jumped so they could punish some of the townies who had harassed them.

MIT: A GREAT NEW HISTORY

Harvard and MIT are a dialectic that never freezes into a synthesis, although one Harvard president wanted to join the two universities. MIT, founded on April 10, 1861, two days before the start of the Civil War, is a world-famous research center and a residential university. It has been in East Cambridge since it moved across the Charles from Back Bay, Boston, in 1916. The construction of the new campus was made possible by the donation of an anonymous person. The identity of "Mr. Smith" was revealed later to be George Eastman, the founder of Eastman Kodak. Some parts of the Institute go beyond the campus and include worldwide affiliates.

An MIT collection is kept in a new museum, not archives, including materials on all aspects from the founding through the present. The museum director, John Durant, observed that the museum tries to do two things: represent the Institute to the world and be the world's window on MIT. "Collections help tell that story. Also, it is an introduction to the world of research and innovation that goes beyond MIT. The first major gallery is now an introduction to the spirit of the place by example, of things that typify MIT, give vignettes of life of the Institute."[18]

1970 Unicycle Club at the MIT Rotunda. *Spencer Grant Collection, Boston Public Library.*

The MIT Museum director observed:

> *MIT Student culture has been known to have no concessions, to be full-on. I think MIT has humanized thanks to a conscious decision to be more like other elite universities. Women have had a civilizing influence. In some residence halls there used to be food fights but not since women students have been admitted.*[19]

HARVARD SQUARE AND THE KIOSK

In the 1830s and 1840s, Harvard Square, with Wadsworth House on its edge, was known as the Market Place. Country produce, especially loads of wood and hay, were brought in nearly every morning for the village supply, with the wagons parking under one of the tall elms. The market proper was a small building in the middle of the Square. From the Cambridge Historical Society's *Proceedings*:

Harvard Square in those days was like Harvard Square today—you could always meet unique people. One day Mary, as everyone knew her, would ask you for a pair of shoes to wear to church in....It was not unusual on a warm spring day to see Professor George Lyman Kittredge come out of his lecture room in Harvard Hall and start to cross Massachusetts Avenue. He did not wait for traffic; traffic waited for him. What motorist would dare keep on driving when he saw a tall, vigorous, white-bearded man—nattily dressed in a very light gray suit that fitted him like a model, hat to match— put his head down, raise his cane imperiously over his head, and charge into the street in front of the car? The only Harvard Square traffic for which "Kitty" would give way was one of those herds of cows frequently driven right through Harvard Square and down Boylston Street on their way to the Brighton abattoir.

Until 1840, the meat market, or butcher's shop, was in the basement of the old Court House, later replaced by Lyceum Hall. There stood a watering trough and hay scales where the Kiosk stands now. Lois Lilley Howe recalled from her childhood Harvard Square and the Yard, buildings and businesses:

Harvard Square, 1922. *History Cambridge.*

Cambridge was still a small college town and had an atmosphere of its own. As a child, I was allowed to go to school or anywhere else without any escort other than a contemporary one. I was sent to Harvard Square on errands; I even disported in the College Yard, which lay between Harvard Square and "our house" on the corner of Oxford and Kirkland Streets. The Square, then, as I remember, had some of the charm of an open space and was not too crowded. But there was one important feature which we never thought even picturesque until it was gone forever—the horse. Horses were everywhere; on the tradesmen's carts, on the ice carts, the express wagons as well as on the private carriages of our more wealthy citizens.

Likewise there were the horsecars....They were low and square and yellow with flat roofs. Each was drawn by two stalwart horses (four when snow was on the ground).[20]

The authoritative (and weighty) *Historic Cambridge* answers many questions about the city's evolution:

The physical fabric of modern Cambridge was essentially complete by 1925. Streets had been widened, paved and lighted, curbs and sidewalks installed, water and sewer lines extended to every neighborhood, the subway opened, and the park system completed. By 1916 almost every house was connected to a sewer, and only a handful still relied on private wells.[21]

As for the Square, it had been vibrant since the beginning. In the 1950s came the transformation of the Brattle Theater into a movie house for foreign films and the Humphrey Bogart film festival; Design Research, with its Scandinavian furnishings and fabrics; and, at Club 47 (47 Mount Auburn Street), a coffee house and folk music venue. Joan Baez, a girl who grew up in Belmont, performed at the Kiosk and used a picture taken of her there in 1959 on the cover of her first album. Later, Tracy Chapman was a performer here.

According to the shoemaker where generations of students have gone for shoe repair, whose shop is at 1301 Massachusetts Avenue across from the Yard, "There's no better place than Harvard Square. Nobody knows how good it was before people were scared to come out and worked at home." According to George Despotes, a natty, slender and gregarious businessman who often chats with panhandlers and with the police who have the busy beat of the Square, "Things get worse—Out of Town News is gone. Things get better—having the Alewife Station is good for people."

As a central point of Cambridge, the Harvard Square Kiosk has had a long history of being remodeled. Soon after it was constructed in 1926, it was discovered that the headhouse, with its oval brick design and Georgian colonnades on two sides, obstructed vision for motorists and presented a hazard to pedestrians. A replacement of 1928 had a thin copper roof of intersecting barrel vaults supported by piers of brick and limestone. It bore signs promising "Eight minutes to Park Street," which caused many jokes about the transport, which creaked and jerked along until it ground to a halt late in Boston.

The Out of Town News was next to the entrance to the subway. When the subway was rebuilt in the 1980s, the kiosk ceased to be its entrance and exit, and the Out of Town News moved into the unused structure, adapted to the purposes of the newsstand from 1981 to 1984.

Architectural critic Ian Nairn characterized the Kiosk in the mid-1960s as "an urban epigram in a tiny space…probably the most important space in Harvard," adding that "the kiosk island, despite the traffic which swirls around it, unites the area and gives it character: Everyone recognizes the newsstand as they would Nelson's column."[22] In the 1970s, the Out of Town News, founded in 1955, was very busy. People didn't linger—they came in and out fast and knew what they wanted. I remember buying a big apple and yogurt at the German fancy food store on the corner and then standing in front of the Coop while my Harvard Summer School classmate, the future father of my twins, bought his daily *New York Times* at the Kiosk. Then we would have a break on the grass in the Yard.

The janitor of the Harvard housing quarters where we lived was a slight, quiet person named Mike Murphy of County Clare. He made friends with several of the graduate students who moved with his large family into a larger apartment in North Cambridge. Mike did not like random chats about his brogue or heritage, but we saw him in Harvard Square one evening, in lively conversation with a professor who, like him, held a copy of the *Irish Independent*. One of his newspapers he read in Gaelic and got at the Out of Town News. It was said that some of the newspapers were flown over daily, but his was a weekly. Being there at that little patch of territory in the middle of Harvard Square made us feel urbane. In New York, an array of sleazy periodicals was carried in newsstands, but in Cambridge you had to go down the street for that. Out of Town News carried more than two hundred newspapers, including *Foreign Affairs*, *The Bengali* or the *Neue Zürcher Zeitung*. It was also the only place to find the *Sunday Globe* real estate classified on Saturday afternoon and get a beam on new listings.

John Kenneth Galbraith walked down from Francis Avenue daily for his *Le Monde*. His neighbor Julia Child came for Italian and German cooking magazines. It is said that Robert Frost once stopped by on a snowy evening to get directions to a reading.

Besides being a profitable location for selling newspapers, the busy crossroads represented the intellectual atmosphere of the city until the market dwindled, the Out of Town News closed down and the city bought the Kiosk to turn it into public space. A historic moment at the newsstand occurred in 1975. A young man bought a magazine that he showed to a friend—simple enough. But the two young men were Paul Allen and Bill Gates, the cofounders of Microsoft. And the magazine was the January 1975 issue of *Popular Electronics* where they read about a primitive personal computer—and it dawned upon them that someday a computer would be in every home and on every desk. "I can still remember grabbing the *Popular Electronics* as if it was yesterday," said Allen decades later.[23]

An ambitious change to the subway came with the new Red Line and a new extension to Alewife. At one point of the excavation, the tunnel had to be dug through 130 feet of bedrock. On the surface, the area affected by the masterplan became a congeries of construction for six years. The masterplan created a new Harvard Square sensible for transportation and of

Harvard Square Kiosk, 1972. *Cambridge Historical Commission, staff photographer.*

The Kiosk circa 2010. *Nasser K.*

benefit to pedestrians. The latest renovation of the kiosk and platform began in 2020 after Out of Town News closed forever.

Preserving the kiosk and giving it meaning in its role of uniting town and gown is now the province of the city. As the kiosk is a protected landmark, new reuse will preserve the original of 1927–28, and the renovations of architectural details—exposed cypress beadboard sheathing and riveted iron structure of the roof, the masonry piers and walls—are preserved. A city-appointed group led a community process to establish a vision for future use of the kiosk and its plaza, and it was agreed that these spaces should enhance the everyday life of the square and act as platforms for community gatherings.

THE KENNEDYS CAMPAIGN

A five-sentence application essay supported the thirty-fifth president's application to Harvard (and came to light in 2022):

> *The reasons that I have for wishing to go to Harvard are several. I feel that Harvard can give me a better background and a better liberal education than any other university. I have always wanted to go there, as I have felt that it is not just another college but is a university with something definite to offer. Then too, I would like to go to the same college*

as my father. To be a "Harvard man" is an enviable distinction, and one
that I sincerely hope I shall attain.[24]

Preferring to go to Princeton with his friends from Choate, JFK in fact enrolled at Princeton and was there from late October 1935 through Thanksgiving. But then he was ill and went to Peter Bent Brigham Hospital in Boston for tests. His father insisted that he follow Joe Jr. to become a Harvard man. (Joe Jr. graduated from Harvard in 1938, left Harvard Law School for the U.S. Navy and tragically died in 1944 while serving as a naval officer.)

JFK chose Winthrop House, the haven of athletes, and for two years was on the varsity swim team. Kennedy's suite from his senior year at Winthrop House in 1939 to 1940 has been preserved and maintained by the Institute of Politics since 1969. Located in Gore G. Entry, it has period furniture and historic photos. Jack shared the suite with classmate Torbert Macdonald, who later was a U.S. congressman. Jack's younger brothers Robert and Edward also lived in Winthrop House, as did Caroline Kennedy (class of 1980).

In personality, at Harvard he showed a cooler temperament than his older brother's. Just before Jack graduated, his senior thesis, which he had reworked into a book, was rejected by the publisher that had wanted it. Once the graduation fete was done, he went to New York to see a new publisher, which offered to bring out *Why England Slept.* This early success got him offers to go to Europe as a correspondent, more attractive than his original place of attending Harvard Law School.

President Kennedy was not only educated at Harvard but also began his political career in Cambridge and maintained a lifelong association with the city. One month before his assassination, on November 22, 1963, he watched the Harvard-Columbia football game and chatted at halftime with President Nathan Pusey.

From 1914 for twenty-six years, Cambridge was represented in the U.S. Congress by Republicans. Then, during the New Deal, a Democrat was elected, a former mayor and the son of a governor, William E. Russell, who had played a major role in the Social Service Administration. He held the office for two years. Apparently, several wards were gerrymandered, making elections volatile. Then came in the prepossessing young Lieutenant John F. Kennedy, fresh out of the navy, whose older brother had been killed and who now took on the political ambition of the family. "Jack" had the influence and financial backing of his father (Harvard class of 1912). Jack's father

JFK campaigning. *John F. Kennedy Library, Boston.*

encouraged James Michael Curley, the incumbent U.S. Representative for the Eleventh District, to vacate the seat and run for mayor of Boston; it has been suggested that Joseph Kennedy did this with money. The Eleventh Congressional District consisted in 1946 of Cambridge, Somerville, East Boston, the North End, Brighton and the waterfront community of Charlestown. This contest was between a popular state representative and future mayor, Michael Neville, and Jack, a very hard worker with youth and zeal, who stood for change.

Joseph P. Kennedy Sr. had gone from Boston Latin School to Harvard, where he was a sportsman and a member of the Hasty Pudding Club. As Charles Sullivan wrote, Joseph Kennedy owned the airwaves, the subway and trolley cards and the billboards (some ninety of them at $9,000 per month). When his Irish American background disadvantaged him, he concentrated on making money and eventually became U.S. ambassador to the Court of St. James. The father's prominence was an element in his son's election but arguably second to intense campaigning and charisma. It may be hard to picture JFK knocking on doors of Cambridge's working-class "three-deckers," but it is reported that he did. Moreover, Boston had

JFK seated at a desk. *John F. Kennedy Library, Boston.*

100,000 veterans voting, and the campaign spoke to women. On June 15, the Saturday before the June primary, Joseph Kennedy hosted a reception, a "tea party" for several thousand women at the Commodore Hotel in Cambridge. Invitations were sent to every woman on the locality's voting list, asking her to meet the candidates and Jack's parents. The Commons was wired for sound, and thousands turned out and were greeted in a receiving line that included Jack, his parents and his sister Eunice. Kennedy carried the district with 42 percent of the vote, twice the votes cast for Neville. Wrote Seth M. Ridinger:

> *Kennedy's regimen quickly became arduous. He woke up around 6:15 in the morning and would be on the streets around 7:00. He often went to the dockyards and factories to shake hands with the workers on their way into work. Accompanying Kennedy one morning, Dave Powers overheard one of the dock workers remark, "If this fellow, you know, gets up at 6:00 in the morning like we do…we're going to vote for him."*[25]

Ted Kennedy in Cambridge.
Spencer Grant Collection, Boston Public Library.

Thomas P. O'Neill, who later took Kennedy's vacated seat in 1952, said that Kennedy as a candidate was a maverick in this regard.[26] And Robert Kennedy succeeded O'Neill in Congress. The victorious campaign of his older brother served as the entry of Robert Kennedy into politics, according to his biographer, Arthur M. Schlesinger. Robert Kennedy was a navy man like his two older brothers. He left Milton Academy at seventeen in 1943 to report to the V-12 Training Program at Harvard (November 1944–June 1945). For a spell he relocated to Bates College (a cheerful photo shows him and other sailors on a snow replica of a navy boat they had built). He returned to Cambridge for six more months of the program. The war had concluded, and he entered Harvard as a junior, with credits for the training program, graduating in 1948.

Robert Kennedy had average grades (Schlesinger noted that his string of Cs was broken only by Ds in Anglo-American Law and the Principles of Economics). He was an ardent athlete and football player, gregarious and principled. Despite being five-foot-ten and only 155 pounds, he won two varsity letters. He belonged to Spee like Jack, but according to Schlesinger's biography, when another Irish American was shut out of the club, Bobby never went back. After graduation, he went to Europe and the Middle East as a correspondent for the *Boston Post* (JFK had been given a job as a correspondent for the *New York Journal American*) but returned to Cambridge to campaign for Jack. Bobby worked focally in East Cambridge, which was more of a challenge. He played softball with kids in the park across from the campaign headquarters.

Next to the Charles is a greensward named the JFK Park created in the president's honor.

CULINARY COLLECTION

The Schlesinger Library at Radcliffe is dedicated to "advancing Harvard's Radcliffe Institute's commitment to women, gender, and society." It has 35,000 cookbooks or food-related volumes—for example, a breathtaking sixty editions of Menon's *La Cuisinière Bourgeoise*, beginning with the first edition of 1746, as well as manuscript cookbooks and two thousand menus spanning more than five hundred years. The core collection came to Radcliffe in the 1960s when it was a women's college within Harvard. Widener was apparently looking for space, and they moved the approximately 1,500 cookbooks then in the library to Radcliffe. Marylene Altieri, curator of published and printed materials, stated that at the time many among feminists involved with the library were unhappy to see the cookbooks come in. Underrating the importance of cookbooks, they thought that cooking was something to be left behind. Since that time, it has been acknowledged by academe that cookbooks contain valuable economic and social history. The Schlesinger's collection has grown as it has bought and been given more rare cookery volumes and the papers of women accomplished in the culinary field, such as the papers and cookbooks of Julia Child. "For a food writer, going to the Schlesinger Library is like visiting an older and wiser friend," according to Jeri Quinzio, author of *Dessert: A Tale of Happy Endings*. "The atmosphere is warm and welcoming. The resourceful librarians are always eager to offer help and advice. Most of all, of course, there are the books. I learn something new every time I visit."[27]

The earliest cookbook in the collection is a 1567 title; the collection includes volumes from the seventeenth and eighteenth centuries, before modern printing changed the way books were illustrated, printed and bound. It contains incunabula, or books printed before 1501; volumes on table manners and etiquette for children; books on carving; instructions for winemaking; treatises on dietetic and medicinal cookery; and menus. Such household books were an indispensable feature of the Renaissance palace, manor house and convent, as well as, by the mid-eighteenth century, the middle-class wife's kitchen.

The menu collection spans the mid-nineteenth century on and contains bills of fare as well, giving an idea how the rich have feasted on banquets of pheasant, lark and apple tart.

Even before the Schlesinger collection became well known, Cambridge was arguably an American center for cookbook authorities. When interviewed for *Connoisseur* magazine in 1982, Professor David Segal said that he belonged to a group of scholars, food writers and broadly educated cooks who met each month for an evening devoted to food.

In April of the previous year, he remembered, the subject was garlic. Everybody brought in some unknown information—a Latin poem, sources on its medical and aphrodisiac properties, something on the invention of the garlic press, a Persian pun and so on. "I wager more scholarship on garlic was presented that night than at any other time or place hitherto. And the room in Adams House was redolent with the garlicky canapés one of the members had prepared."[28]

A frequent guest at the table of Segal was Julia Child, who jested that he was the only amateur cook in Cambridge who dared to have her to dinner. I wondered if they served America's most celebrated cook something homey, say pot roast and corn on the cob, but I've been told the epicures dined on scallops Florentine, julienned carrots, romaine and avocado salad, sorbets and cookies, as well as a Rossigny-Comte de Vaut 1969, a fitting celebration of town and gown.

Professor Gates

On July 16, 2009, Henry Louis Gates—a prominent African American scholar, Harvard professor and public intellectual—returned to his home in Cambridge sick with a cold and exhausted after a twenty-four-hour flight from China. Finding the door of his house jammed shut, he enlisted the driver who had driven him from the airport to help force it open. They next tried a screen. There had been break-ins lately, so a neighbor called 911 and reported that there might be a burglary on Ware Street.

The responding officer was Sergeant James Crowley, and soon he and another Cambridge police officer arrived and Gates was arrested. It was clear that Gates was trying to enter his own property; unfortunately, the climate worsened on both sides. Soon Gates, incensed, and Crowley were on the front porch with onlookers on the scene, and Gates called out to bystanders truthful but not judicious words: "This is what happens to Black people in America."

Gates gave proof of his identity and address but was arrested nonetheless. The charge was disorderly conduct, and off Gates was taken to the police station in handcuffs. But as legal scholars have pointed out, shouting at or verbally abusing an officer is par for the course of police work. Calling a police officer a racist, as Gates did, is within the First Amendment right. However, Crowley, although a seasoned officer who had a career in the university police of Brandeis and Harvard Universities before joining the Cambridge force and had recently taught a course to police about racial profiling, did not make the legal distinction between verbal abuse, being yelled at and disorderly conduct, which according to the law means behavior riling up others. Thus, Gates was charged and held for four hours until the matter was untangled, and he was free to go home. Five days later, the charge was officially dropped.

However, the incident had political ramifications, as Americans debated whether racial profiling had occurred. President Obama, elected six months before, stated that arresting Gates for disorderly conduct committed on his own porch was "stupid." As Obama wrote in his memoir, a poll showed that his approval rating dipped because of his words, and it never rose over 50 percent again among white Americans, thus causing a bigger drop in his support by white people during his presidency than any other single event. I think we can hear the president dispassionately analyzing the scene but overlooking how citizens would take the part of either Crowley or Gates.

One week later, President Obama apologized for his remark but stayed firm in his expression that Black Americans are more often than white Americans arrested or accosted by police officers if perceived as acting suspiciously. In a way that the American public recognized about Obama, he acted presidential, and on July 24, two weeks after Crowley arrested Gates, the professor and the policeman were invited to the White House. They had a private meeting with the president that took place in a courtyard near the White House Rose Garden. This became nicknamed the "Beer

"Beer Summit" in the Rose Garden. *Pete Souza, White House Historical Association.*

Summit." No one knows the precise words exchanged, but the confrontation was resolved. The news reported what was of national interest: which type of beer each drank. Vice President Biden's was of very low alcohol content, Gates had Red Stripe, Crowley Blue Moon and President Obama Bud Light. Gates told the *New York Times*, "We hit it off right from the very beginning. When he's not arresting you, Sergeant Crowley is really a likable guy."

Both professor and police officer were used to demanding respect and to keeping their own responses in difficult situations in control, and yet they handled the confrontation at Gates's home in a hostile manner. The professor could have deescalated the situation, and the policeman could have realized that the 911 call was a mistake. Both came from a culture that made them stiffen with resentment, and their anger flared. At present, Sargent Crowley holds the rank of detective sergeant of the Cambridge police, and Professor Gates is director of Harvard's Du Bois Research Institute.

The Cambridge Review Committee, a committee of experts on police work from across the country, investigated the circumstances that led to the arrest and issued a sixty-page document called "Missed Opportunities, Shared Responsibilities," which found that "misunderstandings and failed communications between the two men" caused the escalation. "For various reasons, each man reported feeling a certain degree of fear of the other," as Crowley responded to a 911 emergency call about an apparent breaking and entering and Gates was "wary of the police" and "did not recognize Sergeant Crowley's concerns or why the Sergeant wanted him to step outside his own home."

There was some humor to the regrettable affair. Gates had a bad cold and maintained that he couldn't have shouted very loud and that a fifty-eight-year-old man with a limp was an unlikely burglar. In the aftermath of the meeting of the police officer and the professor with the president, Gates asked Crowley for a sample of his DNA. When the sample was analyzed, it suggested that they are distant cousins who share an Irish ancestor, the legendary northern Irish king Niall of the Nine Hostages. In a PBS series on African American ancestry that he hosted in 2008, Gates discovered that he was descended from an Irish immigrant and a slave girl.

The result was unique—between an Irish policeman, the local Cambridge police force and a renowned Harvard professor.

THE SEAL

The first iteration of the Harvard seal or crest dated from the 1640s. It was a rough sketch filed away by President Josiah Quincy. The Latin motto was *Veritas*, spelled out on three books. The seal has been very important to Harvard. Today, twelve different schools of the university, from the business school to the medical school, each has a variation of the design. Only the law school's has provoked controversy.

In 1640, out of a population of fifteen to twenty thousand, Massachusetts had only one lawyer: Thomas Lechford of Lincoln's Inn in Boston. Reverend Jeremiah Chaplin noted in his 1873 biography of Henry Dunster that Dunster returned to England after three years in 1641 in disgust, returning to where lawyers had more respect. The current opinion among the Puritans was that the law was a wicked profession. Isaac Royall bequeathed to Harvard College some of his wealth to establish a chair in either medicine or law. Harvard chose law, and the first Royall Chair was established in 1815. Royall's wealth by his own admission came from his Antigua sugar plantations, as well as local farms. Royall brought his family and slaves to Massachusetts after a slave revolt was crushed in Antigua. He and his father, also Isaac, had more slaves than any other household in Massachusetts. Cuba Vassall was enslaved by Penelope Royall Vassall, Isaac Royall Jr.'s sister. The Royall House and its slave quarters can be toured today in Medford. During

John Harvard statue in Harvard Yard, March 1934. *Boston Public Library, Leslie Jones Collection (Snow).*

the American Revolution, dozens of the Royalls' enslaved people were sold to raise money for the evacuees' life in London.

The Royall crest, with three sheafs of wheat, was adopted for the Harvard Law School shield when all the colleges of the university were designated with shields in 1937 (and the shared motto *Veritas*). Eventually, the law school was awakened to the fact that its shield had vastly racist underpinnings. In November 2015, an incident occurred in the wake of an exhibit that student activists created called "art-action," which attempted to draw attention to the school's slavery roots, whereby tape was placed on the crests of Harvard Law School in Wasserstein Hall, and facts were posted about Isaac Royall (black gaffer tape was used so as not to leave residue). By the next morning, an anonymous person or persons had retaliated with graffiti: some of the tape was taken off the exhibit and used to cross out the faces of six portraits of tenured Black faculty. The law school appointed a large committee to forge a new shield. Its design looks like stained glass in black-and-white. It was declared to capture "the complexity, the diversity, the limitlessness, the transformative power, the strength, and the energy that the HLS community, in Cambridge and throughout the world sees in Harvard Law School." Beside the university motto *Veritas* appears *Lex et Iustitia*, "Law and Justice."

Magazine Beach and the Coast of Harvard

The most devastating of instances of nineteenth-century great powers making up international laws to suit their imperialist goals was impressment. A woman near the Atlantic coast could walk out the back door to hang up her clothes and come back to find her husband, brother or father missing, kidnapped for servitude on a British warship. No one in the new United States would have disputed the injustice, but not everyone thought that "Mr. Madison's War" was the proper response.

The Embargo Act had closed American ports to British ships and prohibited American ships from all foreign trade. This affected Cambridgeport, east along the Charles, which never developed as a port of delivery. Instead of an expansion of trade along the Charles River, there were two years of war with Britain, culminating with the British burning the White House, the Capitol and other buildings in 1814. As the British and French each blockaded the other's ports, impressment not only of the occasional native-born or naturalized Americans but also of the crews of whole merchant ships occurred.

Indicative of the importance of the War of 1812 in Cambridgeport's local history is how many cross streets in that neighborhood have the names of war heroes—among others Perry Street for Commodore Oliver Hazard Perry, hero of Lake Erie; Decatur Street for Commodore Stephen Decatur, who reined in and made peace with the Barbary pirates; and Lawrence Street for Captain James Lawrence, secretary of the navy, 1809–12. This was the work of Edmund Dana, who inherited a great deal of land in Cambridgeport. Dismissed mid-winter of his senior year for "absence of prayers" and other infractions of the rules, Dana joined the U.S. Navy. The ship he sailed on limped into Chesapeake Bay, destroyed after its first battle. Asserting that he had been seasick every day of the voyage, Dana never sailed again.

Three years after the treaty with Britain was signed (1818), a powder magazine was built near the shore of the Charles. There was no more armed conflict with Britain, and it fell into disuse. Restored from wreckage in the twenty-first century, the landmark is now an Audubon center. Volunteers in partnership with the Department of Conservation and the City of Cambridge have created a delightful seventeen-acre park encircling that spot whose Olympic-size free public swimming pool has lawns that extend to the Charles. Magazine Beach, with the powder magazine, is located near the Boston University Bridge.

People for the Riverbend Park Trust photo contest. *John and Ellen Moot Papers, Cambridge Room, CPL Archives and Special Collections, Sandra Basley, photographer, 1982, Cambridge Public Library.*

Harvard students have always swum in the Charles, and in the early days some lost their lives doing it. The strong currents ended when the river was dammed. When the river was tidal (until 1909), there were significant currents in the vicinity of the Great (now Anderson) Bridge, and the college repeatedly banned swimming there. In the 1890s, the Cambridge Parks Commission established swimming facilities (with changing rooms and lifeguards) at Magazine Beach, and for fifty years an open-bottom barge was moored for use as a swimming tank. The riverside area became a swimming place that attracted sixty thousand swimmers in season in 1900.

"A simple fall into the water used to require a tetanus shot," quipped Corydon Ireland in the *Harvard Gazette*.[29] By contrast, a fifty-year effort by the Environmental Protection Agency has made the river so clean that most days it is said to be safe to swim in the Upper Charles. In the second half of the nineteenth century, not only did swimming become vogue but also crew became a beloved Ivy League sport. The rampant industrial use ceased as the Charles began to be perceived as a unique civic asset and symbol of the city.

The Charles River really does have a hidden history. Not only is there a fragment of an eighteenth-century seawall on Winthrop Street, but Professor R. Stilgoe, Orchard Professor of the History of Landscape, also pointed out that old maps at the historical society show another creek running into today's Harvard Square (at the location of the Little Red House Restaurant).[30] At that time, the campus was so surrounded by water that it was thought ships could eventually dock at Harvard's gate.

"THE PURITAN"

Samuel James Bridge, an appraiser of the port of Boston during the Gilded Age, donated the sculpture in Harvard Yard of John Harvard, as well as the John Bridge monument, known as "The Puritan," in the northeast corner of the Common, in memory of his ancestor. Samuel Bridge (died in 1665) was active in government and education, but what gave the monument

"The Puritan" statue toppled, 1935. John Bridge monument, Cambridge Common. *Boston Public Library, Leslie Jones Collection.*

The Charles frozen over. *Spencer Grant Collection, Boston Public Library.*

the epithet was a tribute that starts "This Puritan" on the pedestal. "The Puritan" has been toppled several times by, it is believed, students and young townsmen. In 1922, it was found with a rope around its neck, and in 1935 it was found garroted with wire and prone on the cemetery grass. The sculptor was Thomas R. Gould, a Neoclassical artist active in Boston and Florence.

NOTES

PART I

1. *Journal of John Winthrop*, "History of New England," October 21, 1636, 195.
2. Wood, *New England's Prospect*.
3. De Normandie, "John Eliot," 349.
4. Ibid.
5. Dunster abandoned the Puritan infant baptism altogether.
6. Transcription of the Charter of the President and Fellows of Harvard College under the Seal of the Colony of Massachusetts Bay and bearing the date May 31, 1650.
7. Personal communication with a relative.
8. Morison, *Three Centuries of Harvard*, 117–18.
9. Batchelder, *Bits of Harvard History*, 99–100.
10. Ibid., 83–84.
11. Thomas Keeline, Stuart M. McManus, Benjamin Larnell, H. Clarke and Jakob Hendrik Hoeufft, "Benjamin Larnel, the Last Latin Poet at Harvard Indian College," *Harvard Studies in Classical Philology* 108 (2015): 621–42, https://www.jstor.org/stable/44157825.

PART II

1. Andrew Delbanco, "Endowed by Slavery," *New York Review of Books*, June 23, 2022, 59–62.
2. Caitlin Galante–De Angelis is a graduate of the Harvard Graduate School of Arts and Sciences. She was a former research associate for the Harvard and Slavery Project.
3. Merrill, *Sex and the Scientist*, 14.
4. George Washington to John Adams, July 16, 1775, Founders Online, National Archives, founder.archives-gov/documents/adams.
5. Abigail Adams to John Adams, Braintree, July 16, 1775, Adams Family Correspondence, vol. 1, Massachusetts Historical Society.
6. Brady, *Martha Washington*, 105.
7. December 30, 1775, in Fields, *Worthy Partner*.
8. New England Historical Society, "Mrs. Washington Tries to Cheer the Troops."
9. Alice M. Longfellow in the *Cambridge Tribune*, April 21, 1900, quoted in Higginson, *Henry Wadsworth Longfellow*.
10. *American Heritage* 16, "Baroness on the Battlefield."
11. Rashdall, *Universities of Europe in the Middle Ages*, 26.
12. Morison, *Harvard College in the 17th Century*, Part I, 24.
13. *Diary of Timothy Fuller*, class of 1801, Cambridge Historical Society, vols. 9–11, 1915, 35.
14. Ibid.
15. Wordsworth, *Prelude, Or Growth of a Poet's Mind*, Book 3, lines 250–56.
16. *Harvard Crimson*, "Maids Are a College Institution, but Time May Bring Big Changes," November 22, 1950.
17. Drucker, "Kennedy Letters Misplaced."
18. Farrell, *Ted Kennedy*, 17.
19. Day, *Biography of a Church*, 179.
20. Ibid., 26.
21. Letter of Theodore Roosevelt to Martha Bulloch Roosevelt, Theodore Roosevelt Collection, Houghton Library, Harvard University, January 11, 1879.
22. Personal communication.
23. Ann Austin, *Community of Faith Moves the Change*, vol. 2, *The Biography of a Church*, 40.
24. Shipton, "Harvard Loyalists in New Brunswick."

25. Personal communication with Ronald Reese, author of many works, including *New Brunswick: An Illustrated History*.
26. Maycock and Sullivan, *Building Old Cambridge*, 24.
27. Freeman, "Changing Bridge for Changing Times," 28.

Part III

1. Doris Hayes Cavanaugh, "Early Glass Making in East Cambridge," in *Gleason's Pictorial and Drawing Room Companion*, 1851, in *Proceedings of the Cambridge Historical Society* 19 (1926).
2. Alice Dragoon, "Mapping the Changes in Kendall Square," *MIT Technology Review* (September/October 2015).
3. Denton, "Behind the Velvet Curtain."
4. Maycock and Sullivan, *Building Old Cambridge*, 796.
5. Higginson, *Henry Wadsworth Longfellow*.
6. Henry Wadsworth Longfellow to George Washington Greene, March 29, 1832, "Longfellow's Grave Encounter," Allison Ellis, March 25, 2021, blog.pshares.org.
7. Harrigan, "House that Longfellow Loved."
8. Maria Bowen, "Reminiscences of Follen Street," in *Proceedings of the Cambridge Historical Society* 20 (1927–29): 100.
9. Oliver Wendell Holmes, "The Soldier's Faith," an address delivered on Memoriam Day, May 30, 1895, at a meeting called by the graduate class of Harvard University. "The Harvard Regiment," 20th Regiment, Massachusetts Volunteers Infantry, 1861–65.
10. *Harvard Magazine* (May 1861). A letter was tipped into its pages.
11. Harvard College, class of 1865, baccalaureate sermon and oration and poem, HUC6867, Harvard University Archives.
12. Howe, "[Alumnus's] Architectural Career," 21.
13. Maycock and Sullivan, *Building Old Cambridge*, 98.
14. Cummings, *six nonlectures*.

Part IV

1. Dana, *Two Years Before the Mast*, 1.

2. Project Gutenberg, *Two Years Before the Mast*, by Richard Henry Dana, https://www.gutenberg.org/files/2055/2055-h/2055-h.htm.

3. Perry, *Richard Henry Dana*, 347.

4. Charles Eliot Norton, "Reminiscences of Old Cambridge," in *Proceedings of the Cambridge Historical Commission* 1 (1905–6).

5. George H. Hanford, "The Immigrants of Cambridge, Massachusetts," in Abeel, *City's Life and Times*.

6. Irene Linda Gordon is professor emeritus of history at New York University and author of *The Second Coming of the KKK*.

7. Levien, "Crimson Klan."

8. Frederick W. Hamilton, "Ku-Klux Klan," Supreme Council 33rd Northern Masonic Jurisdiction, office of the Deputy for Massachusetts, Masonic Temple, Boston, Massachusetts, January 22, 1923, 28.

9. *Cambridge Chronicle*, April 3, 1918.

10. *Cambridge Chronicle*, "Trees on Common Not to Be Molested," June 8, 1918.

11. Michael Punzak, a performing musician and writer of children's books, taught for many years in Cambridge public schools.

12. Clarence Thomas, speech to the National Bar Association, January 20, 2017, Black Past, blackpast.org/African-american-history/1998-Clarence-Thomas-speech.

13. Maycock and Sullivan, *Building Old Cambridge*, 111.

14. Peterson, *Nightwork*.

15. Personal communication.

16. Andre De Hon, "Mastery Over the Physical World," in Peterson, *Nightwork*, 197.

17. Personal communication with Tom Rush, Yale 50th Reunion, 2022.

18. Personal communication with John Durant.

19. Ibid.

20. Lois Lilley Howe, "Harvard Square in the Seventies and Eighties," in *Proceedings of the Cambridge Historical Society* 30 (1944): 25–26.

21. Maycock and Sullivan, *Building Old Cambridge*, 71.

22. *Cambridge Chronicle*, "Under the Suns Bonnet Our 'Urban Epigram,'" July 27, 1967, quoting the *Observer Review* (UK), July 9, 1967.

23. December 30, 2009, boston.com.

24. Ibrahim, "John F. Kennedy's Entrance Essay."

25. Ibid., 48.

26. Ridinger, "John F. Kennedy," 118.

27. Jeri Quinzio is a researcher and writer on culinary matters and lives in Boston.
28. Merrill, "Cookbook Collection," 121.
29. Ireland, "River Runs Through It."
30. Personal communication from John R. Stilgoe, October 18, 2022.

Sources

Books

Abeel, Daphne, ed. *A City's Life and Times: Cambridge in the Twentieth Century*. Cambridge, MA: Cambridge Historical Society, 2007.

Allaback, Sarah. *The First American Women Architects*. Urbana: University of Illinois Press, 2008.

Basbanes, Nicholas. *Cross of Snow: A Life of Henry Wadsworth Longfellow*. New York: Knopf, 2020.

Batchelder, Samuel F. *Bits of Harvard History*. Cambridge, MA: Harvard University Press, 1924.

Bell, J.L. *George Washington's Headquarters and Home in Cambridge, Massachusetts; Longfellow House—Washington Headquarters National Historical Site*, February 29, 2012. National Park Service, Northeast Region.

Bethell, John T. *Harvard Observed: An Illustrated History of the University in the Twentieth Century*. Cambridge, MA: Harvard University Press, 1998.

Beveridge, Charles, and Paul Rocheleau. *Frederick Law Olmsted: Designing the American Landscape*. New York: Universe Publishing, 1998.

Bevis, D.M. *Diets and Riots: An Interpretation of the History of Harvard University*. Boston: Marshall Jones, 1936.

Boston College Department of History, Boston College Libraries. *Global Boston: A Portal to the Region's Immigration Past and President*. Boston: self-published, n.d.

Brackett, John Quincy Adams. *Baccalaureate Sermon, Oration & Poems.* Cambridge, MA: Welch, Bigelow and Company, 1856.

Brady, Patricia. *Martha Washington, an American Life.* New York: Penguin Random House, 2006.

Bremer, Francis J. *John Winthrop: America's Forgotten Founding Father.* New York: Oxford University Press, 2005.

Brown, Marvin L., Jr., ed. *Baroness von Riedesel and the American Revolution: Journal and Correspondence of a Tour of Duty, 1776–1783.* Chapel Hill: University of North Carolina Press, 1965.

Bryan, Helen. *Martha Washington, First Lady of Liberty.* New York: John Wiley, 2003.

Chaplin, Jeremiah. *Life of Henry Dunster, First President of Harvard College.* Boston: James R. Osgood and Company, 1872.

Cheever, Susan. *E.E. Cummings: A Life.* New York: Pantheon, 2014.

Cummings, E.E. *six nonlectures.* Charles Eliot Norton Lectures, 1952–53.

Dana, Richard Henry, Jr. *Two Years Before the Mast: A Personal Narrative of Life at Sea.* New York: Doubleday, 1949.

Day, Gardiner. *The Biography of a Church.* Cambridge, MA: Riverside Press, 1951.

Emmet, Alan. *Cambridge, Massachusetts: The Changing of a Landscape.* Cambridge, MA: Harvard University Press, 1978.

Evans, G.R. *The University of Cambridge: A New History.* New York: Bloomsbury, 2009.

Farrell, John A. *Ted Kennedy: A Life.* New York: Penguin, 2022.

Fields, Joseph E. *Worthy Partner: The Papers of Martha Washington.* Westport, CT: Greenwood Press, 1994.

Gilman, Arthur, ed. *The Cambridge of 1776: Wherein Is Set Forth an Account of the Town, and of the Events It Witnessed.* Port Washington, NY: Kennikat Press, 1876.

Higginson, Thomas Wentworth. *Henry Wadsworth Longfellow.* Boston: Houghton-Mifflin, 1902.

Hutchinson, Thomas. *History of Massachusetts.* Vol. 2. London: John Murray, 1828.

The Journal of John Winthrop, 1630–1649. October 21, 1636, n16. Edited by James K. Hosmer. Cambridge, MA: Belknap Press of Harvard Press, 1996.

Leaming, Barbara, *Jack Kennedy: The Education of a Statesman.* New York: W.W. Norton, 2006.

Lewis, Brian. *"So Clean": Lord Leverhulme, Soap and Civilization*. New York: Manchester University Press, 2008.

The Loyalist Collection: 1768–1835. University of New Brunswick. https://loyalist.lib.unb.ca.

Maycock, Susan E. *East Cambridge*. Rev. ed. Cambridge, MA: Cambridge Historical Commission/MIT Press, 1988.

Maycock, Susan E., and Charles M. Sullivan. *Building Old Cambridge: Architecture and Development*. Cambridge, MA: MIT Press, 2016.

Merrett, Andrea Jeanne. "Lois Lilly Howe." In *Pioneering Women of American Architecture*. Edited by Mary McLeod and Victoria Rosner. New York: Beverly Willis Architectural Foundation, 2022.

Merrill, Jane. *Sex and the Scientist: The Indecent Life of Benjamin Thompson, Count Rumford, 1753–1814*. Jefferson, NC: McFarland and Company, 2018.

Morison, Samuel Eliot. *The Founding of Harvard College*. Cambridge, MA: Harvard University Press, 1935.

———. *Harvard College in the 17th Century*. Part I. Cambridge, MA: Harvard University Press, 1936.

———. *Three Centuries of Harvard*. Cambridge, MA: Harvard University Press, 1936.

Nathanson, Larry. "Lois Lilley Howe: America's First Woman Architect." In *A City's Life and Times: Cambridge in the Twentieth Century*. Edited by Daphne Abeel. Cambridge, MA: Cambridge Historical Society, 2007.

Paige, Lucius R. *History of Cambridge, 1630–1877*. Salem, MA: Higginson Book Company, 1995.

Palmer, Arlene M. *The Art That Is Glass*. Portland, ME: Portland Museum of Art, 2002.

Perry, Bliss. *Richard Henry Dana, 1851–1931*. Boston: Houghton Mifflin, 1933.

Peterson, T.F., with Eric Bender. *Nightwork: A History of Hacks and Pranks at MIT*. Cambridge, MA: MIT Press, 2014.

Proceedings of the Cambridge Historical Society. 44 vols. Cambridge, MA: Cambridge Historical Society, 1906–79.

Rashdall, Hastings. *The Universities of Europe in the Middle Ages*. Edited by F.M. Powicke and A.B. Emden. Vol. 3. New York: Oxford University Press, 1936.

Roden, Robert F. *A History of the First Printing Press Established in English America*. New York: B. Franklin, 1970.

Sammarco, Anthony Mitchell. *Cambridge*. Images of America series. Charleston, SC: Arcadia Publishing, 1999.

Schlesinger Library. *Historic Cookbooks—Research Guides*. Schlesinger Library on the History of Women in America.

Schlesinger, Arthur M., Jr. *Robert Kennedy and His Times*. Vol. 1. Boston: Houghton Mifflin, 1978.

Sullivan, Robert. *The Disappearance of Dr. Parkman*. Boston: Little, Brown, 1971.

Taylor, Karen Cord, and Doris Cole. *The Lady Architects: Lois Lilley Howe, Eleanor Manning and Mary Almy, 1893–1937*. New York: Midmarch Arts Press, 1990.

White, G. Edward. *Oliver Wendell Holmes Jr.* New York: Oxford University Press, 2006.

Wilder, Craig Steven. *Ebony and Ivy: Race, Slavery, and the Troubled History of America's Universities*. New York: Bloomsbury, 2013.

Wood, William. *New England's Prospect: A True, Lively, and Experimental Description of That Part of America Commonly Called New England*. London: Cotes & John Bellamie, 1634.

Wordsworth, William. *The Prelude, Or Growth of a Poet's Mind: An Autobiographical Poem*. Book 3, lines 250–56. London, 1850.

Articles and Papers

American Heritage 16, no. 1. "Baroness on the Battlefield" (December 1964): 1.

Avi-Yonah, Shera S., and Delano R. Franklin. "Renovated Lowell House Will Not Display Portrait of Controversial Former University President Abbott Lawrence Lowell." *Harvard Crimson*, March 26, 2019.

Baena, Victoria. "The Harvard Indian College." *Harvard Crimson*, March 22011. www.thecrimson.com.

Bell, J.L. "The End of Tory Row." *Boston 1775*, blog. https://boston1775.blogspot.com.

Boule, James. "The Professor, the Cop and the President," *Slate*, September 21, 2006.

Brasch, Frederick E. "John Winthrop (1714–1779), America's First Astronomer and the Science of His Period." *Publications of the Astronomical Society of the Pacific* 28, no. 165 (n.d.).

Cambridge Chronicle. "Trees on Common Not to Be Molested." June 8, 1918.

Cambridge Glass Company. "A Brief History of the Cambridge Glass Company." https://cambridgeglassmuseum.org.

Cogley, Richard W. "John Eliot and the Millenium." *Religion and American Culture: A Journal of Interpretation* 1, no. 2 (Summer 1991): 227–50.

Cummings, E.E. "I and My Parents' Son." *The Atlantic*, April 1952. theAtlantic.com/magazine/archive/1953/04/i-my-parents-son/641159.

Daily Free Press. "Harvard Activists Protest Low Wages." February 27, 2002. https://dailyfreepress.com/2002/02/27/harvard-activists-protest-low-wages.

De Normandie, James D. "John Eliot, the Apostle to the Indians." *Harvard Theological Review* 5, no. 3 (July 1912): 349–70.

Denton, Herbert H., Jr. "Behind the Velvet Curtain: A Look at Harvard's Final Clubs." *Harvard Crimson*, May 25, 1965.

Dimaggio, Daniel. "Support the Striking Janitors." *Harvard Crimson*, October 21, 2002. thecrimson.com.

DiPaolo, Diana, and Patricia Capone. "The Harvard Yard Archaeology Project." *SAA Archaeological Record*, March 2022.

Drucker, Linda S. "Kennedy Letters Misplaced." *Harvard Crimson*, November 6, 1979.

Freeman, Dale H. "A Changing Bridge for Changing Times: The History of the West Boston Bridge, 1793–1907." Master's thesis, University of Massachusetts, 2006.

Global Study, Global Nonviolent Action Database. "Quakers Fight for Religious Freedom in Puritan Massachusetts, 1656–1661." https://nvdatabase.swarthmore.edu.

Harrigan, Stephen. "The House that Longfellow Loved." HistoryNet, May 15, 2013.

Harvard Crimson. "Klan Fills Cambridge with Horrible Manifestations—Opposes Quinn for Mayor—Names Kopey Its Klandidate." N.d. https://the crimson.com/article.

———. "Maids Are a College Institution." November 22, 1950.

———. "The Phillips Brooks House. Formal Transfer to the University—Memorial Mass Meeting in Sanders." January 24, 1900. www.the crimson. com/1900/1/24the-phillips-brooks-house-pth-phillips.

Harvard Gazette. "Collection of Historical Scientific Instruments Continues to Amaze." 2019. news.harvard.edu.

Harvard Magazine. "Missed Opportunities" (July 2010).

———. "Saved from the Flames; Ex Libris John Harvard." https://www.harvardmagazine.com.

History Cambridge. "American Printing—Dunster Street Near Mass. Ave." https://historycambridge.org.

Howe, Lois L. "An [Alumnus's] Architectural Career." *MIT Technological Review*, 1963.

Ibrahim, Samantha. "John F. Kennedy's Entrance Essay Resurfaces Online 87 Years Later." *New York Post*, February 3, 2022.

Ireland, Corydon. "Blue, Gray, and Crimson; 150 Years Later, the Civil War Echoes Across Harvard." *Harvard Gazette*, March 21, 2012.

———. "A River Runs Through It: Harvard's Long and Complex Ties to the Charles." *Harvard Gazette*, October 20, 2010.

Kenney, Michael. "Church Reborn." *Chronicle* 5, no. 2 (2005).

———. "1861: The Civil War Comes to Cambridge." History Cambridge. historycambridge.org.

Knieriem, Declan J. "'Haunted by the War': Remembering the University Hall Takeover of 1969." *Harvard Crimson*, June 7, 1979. https://www.thecrimson.com.

Levien, Simon J. "The Crimson Klan." *Harvard Crimson*, March 25, 2021. www.thecrimson.com/article/2021/3/25/harvard-and-klan-scrut.

Maison des Gouverneurs. "Sorel and the First Christmas Tree in the New World; German Traces in Montreal." House of Major General Friederich Adolphus von Riedesel in Sorel/Goethe-Institut Montreal.

McGinnes, Meagan. "Vikings, Baking Powder and Poets: Boston's Long and Confusing History with Leif Erikson." WBUR, n.d. www.wbur.org.

McKibben, William E. "A Hate-Hate Relationship." *Harvard Crimson*, April 10, 1969. https://www.thecrimson.com.

Merrill-Filstrup, Jane. "The Joy of Cookery Books." *Connoisseur Magazine* (March 1982): 120–22.

Merrill, Jane. "Cookbook Collection." *Connoisseur* magazine (November 1983): 121.

Murphy, Norah M. "The Proud Tradition of Toilet Scrubbing." *Harvard Crimson*, February 9, 2017. www.thecrimson.com.

New England Historical Society. "Mrs. Washington Tries to Cheer the Troops in Cambridge." https://www.newenglandhistoricalsociety.com.

PBS. "The Murder of Dr. Parkman." www.pbs.org.murder-dr/parkman.

Powell, Alvin. "Student Diggers Take Harvard's Roots from Dirt to Display Case." *Harvard Gazette*, November 13, 2008. https://news.harvard.edu.

Raffa, Guy. "George Washington in Cambridge and the Birth of a Nation." *Process: A Blog for American History*, February 22, 2017.

Rezneck, Daniel A. "New Bill in Mass. Legislature Attempts to Establish Innocence of Salem Victims." *Harvard Crimson*, December 12, 1953. www.thecrimson.com/article/1953/12/12/Harvard-president-plays-hero-role-in.

Ridinger, Seth M. "John F. Kennedy: Public Perception and Campaign Strategy in 1946." *Historical Journal of Massachusetts* 41, no. 2 (Summer 2013).

Shaw, Jonathan. "The Plant Prospectors." *Harvard Magazine* (July–August 2016).

Shipton, Clifford K. "Harvard Loyalists in New Brunswick." University of New Brunswick, Founders' Day Address, February 27, 1964.

Skerry, Janine E. "Ancient and Valuable Gifts: Silver at Colonial Harvard." *New England Silver and Silversmithing* 70. Colonial Society of Massachusetts, www.colonialsociety.org.

Subbaraman, Nidhi. "The Evolution of Cambridge." *MIT Technological Review*, December 21, 2010.

Theodor, Elisabeth S. "Four Students Arrested." *Harvard Crimson*, September 13, 2002.

U.S. National Park Service. "Lechmere-Sewall-Riedesel House."

Walecki, Nancy Kathryn. "Rooted." *Harvard Magazine* (March–April 2022): 28–36.

Williams, Victoria. "Great Cake." Mount Vernon. https://www.mountvernon.org.

Woods, Allan. "How a German Mercenary in Sorel, Que., Lit Up Canada's First Christmas Tree in 1781." *Toronto Star*, December 24, 2017. www.thestar.com.

About the Author

J ane Merrill began her writing career in New York City during its heyday as a sanctuary for freelance writers. Now she lives in Mid-Coast Maine, spending summers in Canada on the Bay of Fundy. Jane is the author of articles for fifty magazines and many books, among her favorites to write being those about Aaron Burr's escapades in Paris, the Parisian showgirl's iconic costume, Sir Benjamin Thompson's inventions and Benedict Arnold's life after his treasonous attempt to sell West Point to the British. She earned her bachelor's degree at Wellesley and her master's degrees at Harvard and Columbia. After several years teaching at an international school in Tehran, she returned to Cambridge, where she headed the North Branch of the Cambridge Public Library. She is drawn to create books that are a kaleidoscope of people, time and place.